Hon

Velma Pollard

BRIAN BUNDI
FORM 4 G

⊞ LONGMAN

Pearson Education Limited
Edinburgh Gate
Harlow
Essex CM20 2JE
England
and Associated Companies throughout the world

Carlong Publishers (Caribbean) Limited
PO Box 489
Kingston 10

33 Second Street
Newport West
Kingston 13
Jamaica

Longman Trinidad Limited
Boundary Road
San Juan
Trinidad

© Longman Group UK Ltd. 1994

All rights reserved. No part of this publication
may be reproduced, stored in a retrieval system,
or transmitted in any form or by any means, electronic,
mechanical, photocopying, recording, or otherwise,
without the prior written permission of the Publishers.

First published 1994
Second impresion 2004

Typeset by The Midlands Book Typesetting Company, Loughborough
Printed in China
GCC/02
ISBN 0 582 22732–1

For Joan Riley

and in memory of my parents Ernest and Lucy Brodber for whom community was everything

It is time to plant
feet in our earth. The heart's metronome
insists on this arc of islands
as home.

Dennis Scott

Biography

Velma Pollard is a Senior Lecturer in Language Education in the Faculty of Education of the University of the West Indies, Mona, Jamaica. Her major research interests are Creole Languages of the Anglophone Caribbean, The language of Caribbean Literature, and Caribbean women's writing.

Ms Pollard is also involved in creative writing, and has published poems and short stories in regional and international journals. She has on the market two volumes of poetry: *Crown Point and Other Poems* (1988) and *Shame Trees Don't Grow Here* (1992), and a volume of short fiction: *Considering Woman* (1989). Her novella *Karl*, which won the Casa de las Americas literary award (1992) is included in the book *Karl and other stories* (1994), also published by Longman.

Acknowledgements

We are grateful to the University of Pittsburgh Press for permission to reproduce an extract from the poem 'Home-coming' from *Uncle Time* by Dennis Scott, © 1973 by Dennis Scott.

Authors' Acknowledgements

A fellowship to the University of Miami Summer Institute for Caribbean Creative Writing June–July 1991 gave me the time and stimulation to write the first hundred pages of this novel. I wish to thank Professor Zac Bowen the organizer of the institute and all the fine people with whom I interacted that summer.

I also wish to thank the following friends who read the manuscript at different stages:

Michael Anthony
Elaine Brooks
Beverley Bryan
Pam Morris and
Mary Conde

PART I

Chapter I   David and Edith

'Him sick bad.' That was a stage whisper from the little girl sitting across from them in the passenger lobby. Her companion, only slightly older, made a face which was meant to silence her. She lowered her eyes and continued to regard him with obvious concern. Eventually she gave one of those deep-voiced sighs you expect from someone much older. David composed his face and tried to hide his embarrassment.

Edith was sitting next to the wheelchair, elegant as always in an understated sort of way; shirtwaist dress, low-heeled pumps, salt-and-pepper hair drawn back in a chignon. The absence of hair exaggerated the forehead and gave the face a stern, no-nonsense look. David was carefully dressed; well-cut navy blue trousers, light blue shirt and a tie in blue and black with one of those timeless paisley designs. His shoes, on the foot rest of the wheelchair, were so shiny he could look down and adjust his tie in them. But there was a certain leathery look about his smooth, black skin, and the grimace of pain which the little girl had noticed passed over his face every now and then, creasing his eyes and twisting his jaw. His other hand, not the one on his thigh, shook from time to time as if it, and not the rest of him, had ague. Edith stretched over and mopped his brow mechanically every time the pain forced beads of perspiration onto it.

Soon they announced that the disabled, people with infants etc, etc, should board, and the attendant came forward to propel the wheelchair towards the door.

Two movies and one stretch of sleep later, they were adjusting seats to an upright position to land on the other side of the Atlantic. Soon people were disembarking. The purser said that Edith and David should wait till everybody else had gone, and came himself to help them descend the stairs while a flight attendant took the hand luggage. The going was slow. A wheelchair was waiting at the end of the steps. David thought of people he had seen hop nimbly into wheelchairs, treating them more like rickshaw than ambulance,

3

and wondered about them. He wanted more than anything else not to have to be so dependent. As soon as he was seated, his face regained the uncomplaining look he had perfected. It was a look easily mistaken for ease. A man dressed in khaki nodded at Edith and pushed the chair towards the terminal building.

The same uncomplaining look mixed with one of embarrassment was on David's face in the baggage hall, as Edith identified suitcase after suitcase for the uniformed man. He took them all in a trolley to an officer at the table beyond the sign which said "Pilots, Air hostesses and Diplomats", then came over to retrieve him and the wheelchair. Edith looked tired. She was thinking about the long journey and about the years of hard labour. She hadn't bargained for having to be man and woman when this time came. The customs officer seemed to sense her need and, after poking around in her hand luggage a little, put a mark on the suitcases one by one and motioned them through. David felt pity for her, but more for himself watching her and feeling guilty. He was wondering what kind of God could smite the retirement he had so looked forward to with such a stroke. The little girl from the Heathrow passenger lobby passed with her mother and sister. She gave him a secret look and he waved at her. She covered her face with one hand and gave him a little wave with the other. He smiled this time in spite of himself.

A young woman rushed up out of nowhere and hugged him tightly. 'Uncle David,' she said, and before he could speak, went over to Edith. It was Laura, the niece who had come to meet them. She was hugging Edith and blurting out a thousand apologies for the bureaucratic bungling which made it take so long for her to get in – something about the temporary pass she had to get. She turned to hug him again. 'Oh Laura,' he sighed, with obvious relief.

'Give thanks,' he said.

'Give thanks,' Laura echoed. And Edith, relaxing slightly, smiled at Laura and said hers.

Laura disengaged herself and started walking ahead of the man pushing the wheelchair. She said some words to a porter and continued at a fast pace.

Almost as soon as they cleared the exit corridor, a station wagon, with Laura at the wheel, came around and stopped

under a "No Waiting" sign. The porter piled the suitcases into the back, then tried to look busy while he waited for his tip. The wheelchair man was helping to get David in. He was obviously an expert. Getting into the seat was slow. David was slow, very slow, but they knew he didn't need a reminder just then. The whole thing was accomplished with great finesse. Edith came in beside him. Laura gave the porter a ten-dollar bill and the wheelchair man twenty-five. They beamed and said, 'Irie sister,' as Laura went around and climbed back into the driver seat.

It was still light outside. Through the windscreen, he could see the mountains lying on their huge sides beyond the flagpoles and the coconut palms. A ship was riding at anchor somewhere out there. Awaiting cargo. Cement perhaps. He had been told about that. Somebody had mentioned it in connection with the closing of Rockfort mineral baths where even country people like himself used to plan to have a bath when they came to town.

'Remember Rockfort, Edith?'

'Yes, but it look mash up now.'

'Turn up your window, Aunt Edith, quick!' Laura said, as a cloud of white dust engulfed them.

The station wagon eased smoothly out, skirting the sea, bright in the afternoon sun with its ripples like stress marks on an ECG printout. David's eyes took on a faraway look. His heart lurched against his chest, then subsided to a steady rhythm. His mind ran to his leaving, thirty years earlier. He had not thought then that it would be so many years; five, perhaps, or maybe ten.

* * *

The exit had been far less gentle inside as well as out. He had been a young man then, excited, on the brink of something new and good. He was tired, yes, but not the bone-deep tiredness he felt now after serving so much time in so comfortless a place. That tiredness then had been from the hassle of decisions to sell or not to sell, to give away or to keep. Documents. Birth and marriage certificates, passports. Everything in two, and he was the one responsible for that part of the footworks. There had been the emotional turmoil, too; tearing himself away from family and friends. The sea seemed rougher then. But was it?

5

Or did it merely mirror the spirit in him then as the calmness now might mirror the calmness he had begun to feel? And there had been the foam bubbling as the huge steamer, let free from its cords, eased away from the shore with its cargo of bananas, and children of the empire going home. And the handkerchiefs of all their friends flapping in the morning wind. He had left from Port Antonio one morning. Here he was now returning to Kingston one evening. And it was his evening. Their evening. Just as it had been their morning.

It had been their morning – Edith's and his – embarking on something they couldn't begin to understand. So many others were going, leaving their children with various relatives till they could send for them. Luckily, they didn't have that complication. If they had, they mightn't have gone. Who knows? The motherland had been crying out for labour, skilled labour. That was what everybody said. And the travel agents were saying that nearly anything you could do was a skill. He had built their house himself after he had finished the carpentry apprenticeship. In fact, what made them so much better off than so many in Wood Village was the fact that he could help build or repair a house here and there, while the bananas grew and the yams and potatoes matured.

Edith had gone to Kingston and taken a course in practical nursing the summer they had made the decision. Every country needed those. They might question her qualifications as a teacher, but not that. And true enough, it was a smart move. They hired her immediately, while her friend with the same teacher qualifications had to take people's babies into her house and watch them to make a living.

She had found work long before he did. Him with his trade. Whoever had told him that the trade would be useful had been dead wrong. It was industrial expansion that caused them to call the children of the empire across the sea. It was factories they needed them to work in. What had given him the edge over many others was not the trade, but more general knowledge than the average West Indian without certificates. He had gone to a good elementary school and had excellent teachers. And he had been a great reader.

He had started on the shop floor, and after three or four factories, had retired as a foreman.

They had been in there together then with the hope and the fear of it.

Somehow, now, he felt that he was alone. Inside. Somewhere, somehow, they had lost it. Whatever it was. A kind of deep sharing that made you feel that each of you was a pillar for the other to lean on. Yes, she was there, the most attentive woman on earth and she knew how to help. She was a nurse. But she wasn't there. Inside.

He didn't know exactly when they had lost it. It didn't go all at once. Maybe the new life had been too much for them. And they couldn't share it after a while. Each person was making a special adjustment. Each one was in a different workplace with different pressures. In the early years, they used to talk to each other about it. Every night. And then it got too heavy. He faced a different struggle from her. The anger and discord was personal although the city was the same. Cold and grey. They had had to work out their own solutions. The effort had given a kind of mechanical turn to what had been a deep and close togetherness. He had been thinking about it all the time while he lay in the hospital bed. He had hoped they would be able to find it again. But could they now? He felt that a part of her couldn't help being resentful. Almost as if he had *taken* a stroke, rather than been given it. For it would certainly cramp the style of their settling in. She wouldn't say a word. And he could no longer read her mind in her eyes.

* * *

In retrospect, David felt that he had gone to England to become a child again. A man who is master of his own piece of land, deciding what to plant and when, is out of practice in taking orders. It was something he had to learn again. He hadn't done it since sixth class and teacher Henry with the leather strap – justice. He had thought it would be easy. But it had been just as hard as learning to dress for the weather or save coins for the heater. Then there was the other part, the child saving for one dream after another; house, car, and eventually, return. What could he make of it now, he, so slow and inadequate?

It wasn't nice to be struck down weeks before you returned home after so long. But he knew he should give thanks still.

7

He had spent a lot of the time in hospital wondering whether he would return in a box like Miss Leila, and willing himself not to do that.

Laura's voice woke him from his reverie. 'Uncle D, I hope you don't mind, but I told Mass Charley he could come to see you Sunday morning. That gives you a whole day to sleep off your jet lag. He says he can't wait any longer. Say he spend too much time waiting for you already and can't wait anymore.'

A slow smile enveloped David's face and he shook his head.

'Trust Charley,' Edith said.

'You know that he and I begin school the same day with two piece of slate in Miss Vera school and follow one another right through to third year?' David asked.

'So you told me long ago,' said Laura.

'Syki and Trim,' Edith threw in.

'From I leave, thirty years now is one time I see him. One year, him and Mary come to England and come look for us. Was the year Mervyn graduate, no Edith?'

'Mhm.'

'Well, he says he will be there Sunday morning DV about eleven, so that if you want to go to church, you can go before that. We have a six o'clock service at St John's across the street.'

'Don't worry yourself about me. You and you aunt decide when you want to worship. I will be glad to see Charley.'

David was more than pleased with Laura. She was the daughter of his sister who had died just as her only child was about to finish high school. There hadn't been much mention of a father at the time his sister got pregnant. They didn't expect one to come forward when she died. He had jumped into the breach and taken full responsibility for her school fees and boarding. She was bright. Had got a scholarship to University, and had come to England and lived with them while she did her post-graduate work. Edith had backed him fully in this and loved her dearly. Now she considered them her personal project. You really do not have to have a child, he thought, there are children out there. In this case, he hadn't even had to look. He wondered about her sometimes, though. Was she happy? Didn't she want to get married? She had had a bad experience, but should it put her off all that forever? Maybe she would talk to him about it one day.

Chapter II   Charley and Myrtle

'Maas D! Bless me eyesight! How you do?'

The woman was tall and well built; somewhat on the heavy side. David etched out a rectangle of face from among the flesh that he saw, put a slim body on it and there was Myrtle, Charley's sweetheart, later wife. All that in the time it took for them to hug each other and for her to settle down in the chair next to his.

'Not as good as you, Miss Myrts.' She gave a little chuckle.

Yes, that was Myrtle. That hadn't changed.

'Charley gone to park,' she said.

Myrtle had barely settled herself in the chair when a shout came from the kitchen: 'Myrtle, come back here and talk to me. A long to see you till a short.' Her getting up was almost as slow as David's to greet her had been. Soon he could hear the lively cackle from the kitchen as the two women reacted like school girls to each other's presence.

Charley soon burst through the door. '"I met a traveller from an antique land who said . . ."' and David chimed in: '"Two vast and trunkless slabs of stone stand in the desert," Charley boy, these slabs can hardly stand.'

They fell upon each other, Charley forming a kind of brace for his friend. Charley was ramrod straight and smiling as he always did. As if he didn't have a care in the world.

'You know, Dave, children in school don't learn these things again like first time. But you looking quite well, man. Edith, how you?' Charley was shouting.

'So so,' came the reply, and in two strides he was in the kitchen, hugging her against his waist.

Back on the verandah with David, inevitably the talk reached the illness. David allowed himself to be free with his long-time friend. It was good to be able to admit to being worried, even depressed, to somebody.

'Don't take it so hard, man,' Charley was saying. 'From what I hear, you come a long way.'

'True; and I have to give thanks. But you know how it

9

is. You can imagine how it feel to be looking on when so much is to be done. Just now, the container will come and all the complication to clear it, for from what I hear, that's not an easy thing. I didn't want Edith to have to take care of all of that.'

'I know,' Charley said. 'But don't worry. I have a plan for that. My Pedro is in the customs broking business now and him can handle it.'

'When I leave here, Pedro was barely walking. Now him is a big business man.'

'Is a few years well since you leave, you know. Plenty water flow under the bridge.'

'But I'm glad the bridge is still here. You take a load off my mind, Charley. You must thank Pedro for me. In advance.' He paused to sip coconut water.

Myrtle had brought a tray with two glasses and had placed it on the table without a word.

'Is like old times, eh Charley, except that your drink is a drink and mine is a chaser.'

'I was thinking the same thing,' Charley said. 'But then I figure that after so long in England you might lose the taste for the whites, even if the doctor didn't say that.'

'You have a point. But you see, I know that is him say it.'

'Forget the bloody rum. I myself shouldn't be drinking it. But seriously. Listen here. I have an idea. It mightn't work, but we can try. Next week, Saturday, I want you to come with me to Milk River. You remember Milk River? A lot of people believe in it. A lot of people get better after a few baths in it.'

'I remember it,' David said thoughtfully.

'We going to stay overnight so you can get two or three baths. Is not the length of time, you know. Is the number of baths that matter. In fact, you not advised to stay more than fifteen minutes at a time. The water is so highly radioactive.'

'Well, Jesus turn water into wine. You going to turn it into medicine?'

'You tongue well sharp still. I didn't say it will cure you, you know. I said I would like to try.'

'I have nothing to lose, Charley,' David said. 'I will try it.'

'The least I will get is the drive and some cashew on the Old Harbour/May Pen road. Is thirty years since I see that

10

road, and almost as long since I eat cashew.'

In the kitchen, the women were laughing with an abandon that Edith at least had grown to forget. She wasn't in her own house yet. They were spending a month or so with Laura while they waited for their things to arrive. But she felt comfortable and somehow right. It was enough to be in Jamaica. *Back at Yard*, as the singer said, drinking coconut water on a Sunday morning with her long-time friend.

'Charley is the best thing coulda happen to David,' she told Myrtle. 'Better than any doctor medicine.'

'I think him have a plan, you know. Want to take him to Milk River. I don't know if you ever hear it, but they say that if you throw . . . well, it used to be sixpence – must be ten cents now . . . where the river meet the sea, and go and bathe in the hot water, you stand a good chance of getting cure.'

'I never really hear that, but tell you the truth, I would advise him to try it. It can do him no harm. I myself wouldn't mind go for the drive out.'

'Well, we might as well make it a sort of outing for the four of us.'

That is how come Charley and Myrtle arrived Saturday morning, Charley driving the four-wheeler and explaining that the road might not be all that good.

In no time, they had reached Six Miles and Kingston was behind them. Marshland spread out on either side.

'Ferry,' David said as they approached the police station.

'You memory good, man. Or is it your eyes?'

'Both,' said David. 'The country bus from Woods always stopped here. And you knew that Kingston was around the corner.'

The jeep picked up speed.

'There is something about this stretch,' said David.

'For me too, you know, no matter how often I do it.' The two women in the back seat were unusually quiet, except for the 'Lord, it pretty,' from Edith, and 'Mhm,' from Myrtle.

Six o'clock in the morning even on a Saturday is a special time of day on the road that eventually takes you from Kingston into Mandeville.

There are large mango trees lining the road on either side, and as you get to Caymanas and beyond it to Innswood,

the green of the canefields in the cool morning gives an awesome peace to the atmosphere. That is until you get to the Old Harbour roundabout, already bustling with early morning shoppers and market women who seem to have slept there.

'Charley,' David asked, 'this place was always so busy? I don't seem to remember anything beside a few women sitting with a little safe with Bammie and fry fish on their knees. And that was late at night.'

'You're right. This is comparatively recent. But it's further around the women stay. When we are coming back, you will see them.'

They didn't get cashews till they reached the May Pen railway crossing. It was too early for the fellows nearer the city. Five-dollar packets the size of a middle finger, and ten-dollar ones slightly bigger, dangled by the car window as each one hoped for a sale. But they weren't pushing and shoving and forcing you to buy, the way the orange sellers have done for generations at Bog Walk. They bought four ten-dollar packets, each from a different young vendor, and everybody looked satisfied. Cashew trees were growing in profusion in fields on both sides of the road.

And they didn't go through May Pen when they should have, and Charley, answering David's query, got a chance to explain the marvel of a bypass he had come to take for granted, making such a difference to the speed and comfort of the journey. It was the Bustamante Highway. A mile or so after the intersection where you could follow the signs and double back into May Pen if you wished, they saw the sign "To Milk River Bath", but Charley didn't turn. He said there was another turn later and that he preferred that road.

They turned at the second sign. 'We still have a good way to go, you know,' said Charley. 'Don't let the signs fool you.'

'"Church of the United Bretheren in Christ",' David read aloud.

'That's only the first one,' Charley said.

Twenty yards later, "Kingdom Hall of Jehovan Witnesses" appeared on the opposite side. Another two hundred yards and Edith was reading "York Town Seventh Day Adventist".

'And they have Methodist and Anglican not far from here,' Myrtle said. 'Jamaica has some kind of world record for churches per square mile, you know,' she continued quietly, 'but I don't think we have any record for righteousness.' For some reason, they all found that funny and laughed.

There was banana and cane on either side of the next tract of road, and aged barracks to show that an estate had once been there. David said he didn't remember anything of this landscape. In fact, Clarendon, as far as he could remember, had always been large areas of flat land with little to show beside cashew trees – the plains of Vere, etc.

He found himself staring at mountains piled on top of each other, sloping gently away from or towards the clouds, depending on how you looked at them.

'But Charley, these hills rivalling St Mary's, man. I don't remember anything like this down here.'

'Yes, man. You just weren't paying attention then. All you ever wanted in Clarendon was cashew and orange.'

'You may be right, you know. But it's a pleasant surprise.'

There were signs all along the way with arrows pointing the traveller onward and saying "To Milk River Bath", as if they could sense that anyone who came off the Highway at the initial sign would expect to have reached the place sooner. About an hour after they had left the main road, the buildings loomed large on the right with "Milk River Mineral Bath" written on the main one.

Charley suggested they check in and have one dip immediately, in case the day visitors filled up the place later. They were shown to their rooms and Myrtle announced that she had brought mint tea as a first course for anybody who wished.

'Capital,' said David, stretching for a cup.

'I haven't heard that term in so many years,' said Myrtle.

David was drinking too seriously by then to react. He emptied the cup. 'Capital again, Myrtle. It hit the spot.'

The others were just starting theirs.

A short flight of steps led to the bath, which was something like a miniature swimming pool. Water came out from pipes that seemed built into the rock. David and Edith, in bathing gear, stepped down them, she walking ahead and leading

him carefully. Soon David felt the warm water caressing his body, inch by inch, as he crouched in it holding onto the edge. He didn't know whether it was mind over matter or what, but he felt as if something was infusing his joints, his whole body. Water came into his mouth. He swallowed it.

'I am swallowing a little of this water, you hear,' Edith said.

'I swallow some already,' said David, 'germs or no germs.'

They could hear Charley and Myrtle splashing in the next kiosk. The sign on the door said that twenty minutes was the maximum per bath, but after ten minutes David said he couldn't bear it anymore. They dried off and went back up to the room.

In a little while, Myrtle announced that it was time to go down to the beach. She had taken over the reins ever since they parked in the yard of the hotel. She said they weren't spending any money on food till evening, and that her food was as good as the hotel's, if not better.

The road on the way to the river was unpaved. The four-wheeler ground its way through red earth with amazing ease. Children and adults were walking everywhere as if they didn't expect a motorized vehicle there, and scampered perplexed when the loud horn alerted them.

'I didn't know there was a definite beach here,' said Edith, looking at children and adults in makeshift bathing suits going towards the brown water. 'I don't know what I expected, but not this.'

'Yes, man, they call it Farquahar Beach,' Charley said. He had been unusually quiet so far. The smell of ganja came in whiffs through the windows of the jeep. 'You smell it, David?'

He said 'Yes, man.'

'I think is the major crop this side.'

'So this is the farming that the government talking about.'

'You been really reading the papers, man.'

Small lean-to shops selling beers and soft drinks, and some basic pastry like bullah and bun, stood on both sides of the road. In the largest of them, a Rasta man was sitting keeping watch over bottles of dark substance labelled "Roots Wine". A large notice of indifferent lettering announced the contents of the drink and its mostly aphrodisiac properties.

14

The jeep came to a stop in the cool of the intertwined branches of some prickly trees. Branches grazed the canvas top like overgrown fingernails. They could see from there a bank of sand at the place where the river met the sea. A young man came up immediately and offered to sell them fish. Charley told him that they didn't need fish and he left. As soon as they had disembarked, he returned and indicated that he knew where they wanted to go. He said he helped people to reach it every week.

'Take you time,' he told them. 'This brother here (pointing at David) look a little weak. If you give me a smalls, I will help you take him up there.'

'OK, Boss,' said Charley, as they walked towards the bank.

The bank was firm as if human hands had made it. It was the colour of the sand they knew. Not black like the sand on the beach they had left. At the water's edge, Charley brought out the ten cents and told his friend what he had to do. Myrtle had the bright idea that everybody should just do it too, for they had nothing to lose. Before they could think, she produced three additional coins.

'Good idea,' said Charley, taking his. 'The sick will get well and the well get better. In any case, who knows what sickness any of us have? Mass D here only have the advantage of being diagnosed. Dash the money in and let us go and eat.'

'A can sell you something, Boss?' the self-appointed guide said, sidling up to Charley, who looked at him and got his meaning immediately.

'No, thank you, friend. I don't use it,' he said. When they got back to the jeep he gave the man a ten-dollar bill and wished him well.

Myrtle had brought everything. Blanket to spread out, folding chairs to sit on, even tooth picks to dislodge any stray piece of saltfish. It was a Jamaican breakfast: chocolate tea in a flask, bammie, ackee and saltfish, obviously put together without regard for what any doctor might think. After the meal, they sat with their knees bunched up or reclined on their sides on the blankets and tried to talk thirty years away.

David told Charley that there were baths in England, but that somehow a Jamaican countryman like him would never

15

think of making use of them, and a friend of his like Charley wouldn't think of suggesting it.

'Anyway,' he concluded, looking at a sheet of paper he had taken from the front desk, 'they say here that this water is nine times as active as Bath in England, so I haven't lost a thing.'

'Good. And I believe they mention your sickness on the paper,' said Charley.

'Yes, man,' said David, touching a folded sheet in his shirt pocket.

'You know the story of the baths?'

'Not yet, but I intend to read the whole brochure.'

'But why you wouldn't go to a place like this in England?'

'It seems like England was made for work when it comes to black people, and that rain and cold comes with it. A luxurious thing like stretching your body and stretching your limbs in some warm medicinal water doesn't have any place there. At least, not for us.'

They relaxed on the beach for a couple of hours drinking Myrtle's ginger beer when they got thirsty. A man passed selling fudge and icicle, and they all wanted fudge to remember way back when.

When they returned to the hotel, the place was crowded. Outside beyond the car park there was a queue. People were filling containers from a pipe at the base of a tank – water they would take away with them. There were others waiting on benches to get to the baths. These were people who came just for the day or to take a bath and leave. It was unbelievable that there could be such a change in what the place looked like after such a short time.

They went to their rooms to shower and change, then went to sit in the little lounge that served the suite they occupied.

'Charley-boy,' David said, 'I don't know if the water can cure all the things they say it can cure, but I know it's good for me. I really appreciate your thinking of it. I believe I going to want to come again.'

'Feel free, man, anytime. Just say the word and I am at your service.'

'Thanks. I will take you up on it. You know, a man in a

16

health food store in England had told me that most of the body's ailments have to do with tiredness. He might have a point. The water like it moving in my bones taking out the tiredness. I had said I have enough tiredness after thirty years work there I thought it might take thirty years rest to undo it. I feel this going to shorten the time.'

Chapter III   Woods Village

There was nothing on the finger post that said which road led to Woods Village. It said "Palmetto" on the body, and on one side of the cross-beam, "To Daggers Run". The other, by default, must point to Woods. The road would become uneven, so that you put your tyres on it at your peril. The occasional paved rectangle only served to disconcert the wheels as they adjusted themselves to the flat roughness of an unpaved road. A few yards in was the fording with nothing but large stones to keep the water out when there was too much rain. It was mostly dry, though, so the stones became just another irritant if you thought about the underbelly of a low-slung car. If you drove a four-wheeler, you could ignore all that and listen for the murmur of the water trickling down into the gully, and the footsteps of children passing on the bridge, undisguisedly fascinated with cars in general and your car in particular.

A slight ascent, two deep bends and Woods proper came into view. There used to be a gas station there and two large shops, one owned by Mr Williams the chinese shopkeeper, the other by Mrs Buckler, a clear-skinned woman with too many children. Men were always playing dominoes in her shop and idlers were always sitting on the piazza. Not so with Mr Williams' shop, though.

'Laura, what ever happen to Mr Williams? The shop look like it lock up long time.'

'Yes, Uncle D, is over twenty years since they leave round here and settle in Kingston. Ah Foo have big hardware business over there, and Mr Williams and Miss Monica helping him. Nobody ever really manage to keep up the shop. Every now and then somebody rent it and try, then they give it up, say it not making anything. And although you see the tank there, no gas has been in it for the longest time.'

There was no need to ask about the other shop. A few uprights still stood on the spot where it had been, but the

building was gone. And the garage behind it where the big bus marked "Kingston to Woods Village" used to park was gone as well. The days of Miss Winey waiting for the driver with her favours were gone too.

'Laura, what happen to Miss Winey?' Edith asked.

'I don't think she lives around here again, you know, Auntie. Her mother lives alone in the old house. At least, that's the last thing I heard. It's really bad, but I haven't checked up on half the people I should.'

'Don't be too hard on yourself, girl. You carrying a lot,' David said.

Up the hill overlooking the little centre that had been the village square, the Willis' house stood out in splendour, its shining water tank picking up the morning sun. The long, well-kept walkway was the first sign of prosperity since the road branched at the finger post. The back of the Niva in the garage was barely visible from the road.

'Mass Ben still going strong?'

'Yes, and Miss Dor too. I hear that one of the children want to come back here because Mass Ben really can't manage the land.'

David hadn't said it, but he had begun to feel depressed since they started the home stretch. But Mass Ben's house looked prosperous as if a man his age (for Mass Ben was older than he) could live in some sort of comfort after all, if he had a little money.

One other bend took them to where the church came into view. The driver stopped. If you know that road at all, you know the view from there is the best. It is the place where the rose apple trees seem to be for ever falling off the hillside, but never fall. Here is where the terrible galiwasps are supposed to live. If they bite you and get to water before you, you are sure to die. But no one had ever seen a galiwasp or could tell what it looked like, and no one had ever been bitten by one, either. The lack of evidence supported the fear, generation after generation.

There was the church, the school that had been new when they left, and behind both, the hills, blue here too, and undulating, eventually touching the sky. Tourists would definitely buy this picture if somebody put it on a postcard.

If you take your eyes off the view and look down on your left to where the hillside seems to be flaking away, you will see a hut. A few sticks really, thrown together and covered with thatch, but not enough.

A woman was standing in the doorway of the hut. Her hair was parted in the centre and two plaits framed her face. They were not fresh plaits. The coiffeur was at least a week old. Her blouse was covered with brown stains, banana or guinep, but it was obviously newly-washed.

'Uncle D, you remember Avis, Miss Betty daughter?'

'Mhm, why? She and you no used to play in holiday time?'

'Mhm. That's her at the doorway of the hut, you know.'

'You mean that *was* her.'

'You're right, for she hardly understands anything of what's going on. After she passed third year, her aunt in England had sent for her. Nobody knows what happened over there, but this is how she came back. And her brother who they sent for too is in a madhouse over there. Same thing happen to Miss Gerald son. People round here say anybody go to England come back mad.'

'Well, let me tell you, my dear, I wouldn't doubt that, and if I find out that I am mad too, I wouldn't be surprised. Is not two pence worth of life over there, you know. The white people them not easy. You have a hell of a time to live with them and still remember that you are a person. You shouldn't even look on them hard if you want to keep you sanity. Is a good thing me and Edith was big people when we went. But why am I telling you of all people and you have first hand experience?'

'I wonder how come nothing happen to the people who go to America. And is white people there too.'

'We don't know. I don't really know. Many of them come back? We never had anybody much from around here going to America to stay. At least, not in my time. I don't think farm workers can stay longer than three or maybe six months. They might go back again, but they spend a lot of time at home in between. And they don't take them after they reach a certain age. You see, America call for visa and all that, because they not part of what used to be the British Empire. Up there, you know, they used to call us King George's blacks.

'The young people you mention were children when they went to England. Maybe they just couldn't stand it. Is too much things to get accustomed to one time. Is the coldness outside. And inside. Then they might go to school, and can't understand the people twang and the people can't understand them. Might be the teachers don't like them, just like how some of the boss dem didn't like us. You will never get to the bottom of it. We just have to give thanks for those who come back here in their senses and pray for those who lose theirs.'

*   *   *

First Sunday is Parson Sunday at the Anglican church in Woods Village. He is really the rector at Highgate, but he is in charge of umpteen churchlets in far away districts to which bad roads lead all over that part of St Mary. On the other Sundays, lay preachers, who Miss Edith used to call "dem bwoy" in her heyday, get the chance to deliver a sermon and expand upon texts they know little about. Some children sleep and others go to the toilet two or three times during the service. Adults who know a little better marvel at the interpretations of the texts and laugh at them in the week over bridge or checkers. At least, that's how it used to be.

The rector used to be white and would arrive with his family or with just his children, whose mosquito-bitten legs would be running up and down before and after church, while local mothers shouted at their children not to play in their good clothes.

Things had changed. Rector was young and black. He expected David and Edith. He had been told that the son of that family represented in plaques on the wall in the church would be coming home from England to re-settle in the district. He said he was glad. Something needed to be injected into the district to get it back to how people told him it used to be. Part of the problem was the poverty now that bananas had been virtually taken out of the hands of the poor. Only rich farmers grew bananas for export now. The demands of the crop were too high now.

Coming through pass Chovey when he went to town, Rector could see large fields of bananas covered with blue plastic bags, obviously beyond the pocket of the little man. And he had seen a documentary showing them being transported to the wharf, already set off in oversized wooden trays. David could have told him about the market in England and how it had changed. How the consumer had become choosy. The standard of the import now had to be higher. And in America, the competition with Latin America was killing the Jamaican product.

Time was when you could stay anywhere in the district and hear the *thwack-thwack* of the sublejack on the back of the mule who dared to bend its knee under the weight of the bananas it was made to drag up steep hill roads all over the parish. That was before trucks took the load to the siding. None of the load went to siding now. Higglers bought it at the gate. They put carbide on the bananas to make them ripe quickly and took them to the market. Of course, the daily pot depended on the green ones. But that steady income from the sale of six or seven bunches a week was gone.

Any little money this family might pay for services, to hire one or two people in odd jobs, would make a difference. And from all he heard, the man was literate. One more lay-reader would relieve Mr Sam, who felt forced to come from Bluefields two Sundays a month whether he was feeling good or not. And he wasn't really well.

*   *   *

The church yard was well-kept, but the terrain was uneven, the way it had been all David's childhood. The almond tree with its heavy bark and its roots halfway out of the earth was still standing, and a few freshly fallen leaves and nuts were under it. You could never really clean the space under an almond tree for more than five minutes. Something was forever waiting to fall. Tomorrow at recess time, the breaking would begin and children would pry open shells with stones and enjoy the brown and white almonds inside.

David wanted to go to see the graves of his parents. He had sent money every month to Zeeland for the upkeep of the space around the tombs. He wanted to see them for himself.

He would have to chance it alone. Mrs Brownen from Rock Spring had collared Edith and would surely not release her in a hurry. He had been walking strongly these last few weeks. He didn't know if the mineral water was responsible. Suddenly he felt that he might fall. This ground was not like the concrete yard he had got used to. He went slowly at first and then with more confidence. He made it.

"Sacred to the memory of . . ." The tombs looked fine. He would stop and thank Zeeland after church and give him a smalls in addition to the shirt and shoes they had brought for him. Everything seemed so long ago. Perhaps it was time to redo his mother's tomb and make it a garden one. She had always liked small flowers, and now he was home to care for it, he might get some rambling roses growing and perhaps a few forget-me-nots. Paa would be quite satisfied with what he had. No trouble there. Just like how he used to eat; not enough salt, eat it all the same; not enough sugar, drink it all the same. A little re-inking of letters on both tombs might be in order. The organ was beginning to play those first few warming-up tunes and the bell was ringing. Service was about to begin. An involuntary shudder came over David. His mother had played that organ all through his childhood.

They didn't go up front to where the family used to sit. They sat near the door in Aunt Joan's pew. She would never sit there again except for a miracle. Her legs had given up. The benches felt very low. The place looked clean but almost dingy. Rat bats still raced each other in the ceiling and peeped about near the pulpit. Edith was already thinking that the altar needed to be dressed the way it used to be when they lived there, and in her mind she was starting up a girls' group attached to the church so they could learn something and also make the church their project. She didn't intend to sit around and rot. Later they would visit the house. Laura said the men had finished the renovation work. They only had to look now and figure out where to put what. She wanted to have a little chat with Mass Zee to see what arrangement they could come to about starting up the garden. David was dead set, she knew, on using up most of the land around the house for vegetables and to try to revive the orange grove, but she wasn't going to let the flowers get left out.

Charley true to his word had got Pedro to clear the container.

Edith hadn't been paying attention. Letting her mind stray. Now she couldn't find where the parson had reached in the service. She had to say the general confession at least, if she wanted to take communion, and she did want to take it. God had to be thanked properly for bringing them to this.

'The gifts of God for the people of God,' the priest intoned, holding the host at chest level. She had missed the confession. Now they had taken the grumbling out of it, you couldn't even recognize it. No more "acknowledging and bewailing our manifold sins and wickedness". No more "the remembrance of them is grievous unto us/the burden of them is intolerable", etc, etc. Even these gifts of God. What happened to "Draw near and take . . .?" Edith's face showed a slight annoyance. How come they could keep the same words in England, where the church was born, and not in Jamaica? Luckily, they were sitting far back. She closed her eyes quickly to say as much of the prayer as she could remember. David had obviously been keeping up with it and was sitting waiting for the light tap at the end of the pew.

The young reverend had lost her just after they were asked to stand so everyone could acknowledge them. The sermon then took off about all the Jamaicans who had ever gone away to look for work, and all those who had lived to return, particularly from Panama and Cuba. She wasn't surprised that David seemed to be lapping it all up. He was a kind of historian himself. He liked that sort of thing. Apparently, some Jamaicans had even gone to Ecuador. The young reverend was obviously learned. She had always thought the poet, Louise Bennett, had invented Ecuador so the lines could rhyme: "Solomon Grampa gone a Ecuador/lef' him wife and pickney out a door". Now she couldn't get that tune out of her mind. She would have to in time for communion. She tried to superimpose "And now, oh father/mindful of that love". She closed her eyes and tried to see David's mother sitting at the organ and a full choir in attendance. That must be the point at which she had reached the yard and the renovation.

At the communion rail, people were standing. That too was

new, but no one seemed to care that they were accustomed to kneeling. There wasn't a kneeler in sight. Some people were actually holding on to the wafer and dipping it in the cup when the wine came around. She had heard about that somewhere. Roman Catholic, perhaps, when she used to hang out with Bibby at school. Thank God a reasonable number were doing what she was accustomed to.

Lemonade and biscuits were served in the vestry after church. This was definitely a new thing. Miss Bel told her it was because some of the members lived so far now – old Woodians who had moved away from the district, but who insisted on worshipping there. If it wasn't for them, there would hardly be a service. The congregation had dwindled down almost to nothing. Some people said it was because the young people didn't come back after they went away to school. But that couldn't be the reason, for there were other young people around. The change was deeper than that.

For years, the Anglican was the established church in Woods. That meant that the teacher and the sanitary inspector, and nearly anybody else who could read, belonged to it. They could read, they had jacket and tie, and they had shoes. If you didn't have those, you couldn't come to that church. A whole set of other people used to go to Mother Lue's Church on the hill, where drum and tambourine made the service lively and where Sunday was not the only church day. A few people belonged to the Jehovah's Witnesses and a few would go to the Seventh Day church at Bluefields.

After church, as they went through Woods on the way over to the house, Edith and David were talking about the decline of their church. When they reached the level, they could see the hilltop where Mother Lue's church used to be. Most of the trees were gone. You could see the structure clearly from the road. It was no longer a thatch-roofed, wattle-and-daub building. It was concrete now, and unfinished, so you couldn't tell exactly how large it would be. Edith looked at the building and remembered the nights when she and her friends would disobey their parents and follow the drums to Mother Lue's hilltop on their way back from the post office. Who was to tell how late the post man had come from Troja? There were all kinds of reasons for his tardiness: train late,

bicycle puncture, and you simply had to wait if your parents were to get their letters and the *Daily Gleaner* coming through the mail two or three days late. And the excuses were still available on the nights that he was early.

The church in America must have sent money to build it up. It wasn't possible for any collection from the people in Woods to pay for all that building material.

Edith's memory went to one night in particular when a foreign parson was visiting. She even remembered his name – Brother Stramm from America. She was squelched in between two poles in an extremely uncomfortable position, but she would rather die than miss it. As the drums throbbed, he passed into the hut like a great black bat with white face and hands painted on. In retrospect, she realized he might have been wearing a simple graduation gown from any school in America. She started to laugh.

'What sweet you so?' David wanted to know.

'You remember the crusade that Brother Stramm came here to start?'

'How you mean? You forget that me and Marshall were there the night you mother nearly kill you?'

'I just thinking that the gown Brother Stramm was wearing could have been an ordinary graduation gown and nobody here was the wiser. I only know it was very frowzy and I nearly suffocate when he passed through the door, for I was literally under his arm. I remember thinking that he looked like a great parson John Crow, and that I didn't believe Bulwark really got any spirit. You remember how he was spinning, and how they couldn't get him to stop and go back on the drums?'

'Remember, yes. All the same, I take my hat off to Brother Stramm. I am not sure I could pull it off if I was him. I am trying to think now where he slept the night; in whose house.'

Ignoring his attempt at recollection, Edith continued.

'You remember Mother Lue's speech?'

'You mean how Brother Stramm never need to come, him coulda stay in America in him rocking chair, just a rock and a rock?'

They were both in stitches. The incongruity of the whole thing had taken them over.

26

'Seriously though,' Edith was saying, 'Brother Stramm or others like him must have come several times for them to have a church like this now. And there is really no reason to come and sit up straight in the Anglican church singing in minor keys if you can shake your body up here in the name of the Lord.'

'And maybe black people not really happy with the "body and blood of Our Lord Jesus Christ", and rector alone talking, and you don't have a chance to answer. You remember how everybody shook and moved about, and said "Praise the Lord", or put in a little unknown tongue?'

'Hektelevan teletengeleng joy,' they both pronounced at once.

'Like it or not, something different from our time is happening. Myrtle was telling me that the Anglican church has been trying a little jigging, too. Creole mass and dance near the altar at Easter.'

'I don't know if that wine can fit into those wineskins. The Catholics have this charismatic thing too now, which is really Pentecostal Catholic. They are talking in tongues too, I hear.'

'From Latin to unknown tongue, well yes.'

'But the whole pentecostal thing – is not only here, you know. I was reading somewhere that it is the whole region and that there is American politics behind it. That's why there is so much American money in it. Tell you the truth, when I read it, the last place on my mind was Woods. I didn't make the connection at all. They were saying that you could trust the Americans to discover what they can work on, and that they were conquering quietly here, without arms; like high blood pressure, the silent killer.'

'That's a serious comparison, man.'

Chapter IV   Returned residents

Looking at the boxes piled on top of one another, Edith remembered the exact feeling she had had when she was packing them. She had felt herself hoping then that June would become September, that she would have moved from an organized house in England to an organized house in Jamaica, and that she would have no memory of the days intervening. The dream had ended. Here was reality. She was now faced with this task which had been like a bogeyman round a child's corner.

Laura had arranged one bedroom. That was the most sensible thing she could do. She had come with them on the Saturday and organized a fridge with food, a broiler oven and an electric kettle. What a blessing Woods had got electricity!

'Trust Laura,' Edith said, when she saw it. 'The girl thinks of everything.'

She had moved enough times before. Not just the big one from Jamaica to England, which involved more giving away and throwing out than packing, but from one flat to another, and later to their own place, in Birmingham. She hated moving. There was always, for her, something frightening about the act of packing and something equally frightening about the act of unpacking. Each became a double action. For as she packed, she couldn't help thinking of the unpacking that lay somewhere ahead of her as she labelled the boxes carefully to lighten the later job. And when finally she got to unpacking, the whole horror of the packing would come back to her as if every item she took out had only just been put in.

But anyone watching her at either end of the business would only get a sense of how organized she was, and would feel nothing of the inner panic she felt every time.

She started with linen tablecloths and napkins to put in the press which was the only thing that had been saved for her from her grandmother's house. She hadn't been around to

put stockings on the old lady's dead feet as she had promised, but the others had remembered that the press was to be hers. She would have liked to put in it the same dried Khus Khus root she remembered from her childhood. It was a smell that was with her all the time now. But nobody seemed able to tell her where to buy Khus Khus, so she had settled for the lavender pot pourri she had found in the mall. The trouble with all this was how much memory the exercise brought back.

The demi-press was in a corner of the dining room. In her grandmother's house, it had been simply the press and stood in the bedroom, easily visible from the four-poster with the rolled bolster, in which they would hug each other, till her grandmother's snores told her that she was alone.

Now every cloth, every napkin she put away reminded her of a friend or an occasion somewhere in her recent past, and thoughts of her grandmother and the smells of her room slid in and out of each memory, making a curious sort of tapestry with unlikely patterns juxtaposed to each other. One moment, she saw the slats of the wooden projection where the large flowered enamel goblet and basin sat off to the left of the press at Comfort Hall, and another, she saw the girls from the hospital sipping a cup of tea at the kitchen table in Birmingham.

They never understood why she was so into tea. They never thought that people anywhere beside England drank tea. Even the West Indians found it strange. Most of them. She used to tell them that if the British hadn't brought tea to the islands the Chinese would have, eventually.

She could hear the intermittent noises from the outroom next to the kitchen where David was unpacking his carpentry tools. God had been good. In the month, he wasn't perfect but he was able enough to begin his unpacking, and wise enough to sit down or to rest when it seemed to be too much. And when he walked, he only dragged one leg ever so slightly. Between the Milk River Bath and the physiotherapy sessions, she didn't know which one to praise more.

And David sat there slowly putting away tools, but coming across the occasional packet of dominoes and remembering the fellows who would join him to recapture a little bit of

home. That was how he came to know about the Caribbean and to feel the brotherhood that sounds like nonsense sometimes on politicians' tongues. The fellows used to say that, since everybody in England thought they were Jamaicans, they might as well get to know them well.

So now everybody knew ackee and saltfish, bammie and fry fish from playing at his house, and he had become a Sunday morning souse man. For some reason, he had not been able to deal with black pudding. And it couldn't be just the blood, for he was accustomed to the sausage from Jerk pork in Boston when he used to visit his brother. Something about the extent of it coiled up on a plate was not for him.

If it hadn't been for those boys, he didn't think he could have made it. The discussions at the tea break, morning and evening, the unwinding over dominoes on the weekend at home, or more frequently at the West Indian Community Centre, gave him strength to tolerate the pressure of the other days. He was wondering, as he had so often wondered before, whether he had made the right choice; whether he shouldn't have braved it out at home, like Charley, for example. Not that he didn't realize the difference in their situations. After all, Charley's father had left him two trucks, at a time when truck was just beginning to take over from cart, to take bananas to siding. Maybe he and Edith had been a little too adventurous. England had looked good from afar. People who travel and return never tell you the whole story. The truth was that the people who had returned had not really been to England. They had gone to war, in the RAF for example, and had pictures of themselves in uniform in their living rooms. Even Mass Nate, who would walk about on Poppy day with his medals and talk about the trenches, though he was clearly in the lower ranks, made the travel thing sound exciting. They couldn't tell you the whole story because they didn't know it.

He had had the stroke the very day after the farewell drinks and speeches at the factory. Perhaps it was shock that caused it. He couldn't believe the speeches they were making because he was retiring. Most of them thought he was too proud for a black bastard anyway. Never asked them any favour. He had worked next to these fellows for ten

years. He had watched some of them come there green as grass and he had taught them the ropes. Somehow, he had thought they would have been different from the fellows in the other factories. They were the same. Talk to you, ask you to show them everything, joke with you up till quarter to twelve; and at quarter past twelve, cut you dead in the cafeteria up the street: 'Hi Jim,' and Jim wouldn't hear you, no matter how loud you shouted. Later, in the factory, you would ask, 'What happen, man, a call to you outside and you didn't answer.' 'What, me? You must be joking. I didn't see you at all.' First time, you believed, although it was really unbelievable, and then you caught the pattern. So next time, before your hand should freeze in the waving and your teeth hold back your lips in the 'Hi', you just held yourself in check and stopped bothering with them. Nobody would believe they could make those speeches and not expect lightning to strike them.

They didn't believe in lightning.

David was thinking he didn't know if the sacrifice had been worth while. Charley looked like a young man to him now. Or so he thought. He couldn't put his finger on what he had gained from all the years he had spent. It wasn't as if they had had a whole heap of children to see through school or anything. True, they had property now. Laura had been in charge of their buying a townhouse in Kingston, and between the rent for that and the pension both of them were getting, they wouldn't want for anything. And he should be grateful. It had been a very near thing. Suppose he hadn't lived to come back? Of course, he wouldn't have known. And he had begged them to send him back, not bury him there. He had had enough in the bank to take care of passage and funeral, and more. He was back alive and was feeling so much stronger already. Almost as if just being back in this country was medicine. Of course, there was the Milk River water . . .

He could hear the press door squeaking on its hinges as Edith put her things away. He could imagine the care with which she was putting each item in place. Such a meticulous woman. And a good woman, too. But again, he was thinking about what he thought they had lost. Not just the laughter.

They used to laugh a lot in the early days. But all of that seemed out of place in Birmingham. Maybe she used to laugh with the girls now and then. The domino crowd and the card crowd certainly used to laugh. But there had been so little time together. When she wasn't at the hospital or out on private duty, she was teaching children to play the organ, just like at home. Except at home she had been a teacher and she had had holidays and free time after school.

And he himself used to do home repairs for the Jamaican community. Everybody knew he had a good carpenter's hand.

By the time they got together, they were so damned tired it was hardly worth the while. So they had lost that as well. And the talking. Lord, how they used to talk in the old days. Maybe what they were going through in the mother country was so bad it was unspeakable. What a mother!

The shed was looking like his already. He wasn't sure what he would do with the tools, but he knew he had them. One thing he had learned in England was how to make small pieces for the house – a stool here, a stool there. He hadn't bothered with those before, just the carpentry. But now he could say he was a self-made cabinet maker. The things in the store had looked so expensive he decided to try his hands at one or two small pieces – a stool for the organ first, and little benches for the children who had to wait to sit on. Eventually, desks that they could do their homework at. And Edith really appreciated those things. She never could be sure when the hospital would ask her to do an extra hour, and she couldn't exactly tell them that children were waiting for music lessons.

Sitting there, he suddenly realized there was something he could do. The way his heart leapt made him understand that one of his biggest and most secret fears was the fear of being useless. After all these years of working every day he wasn't sure he could face that. He could make some chairs and desks for children in school. Bet your last dollar they didn't have enough of those. He would talk to Janet, who was head teacher now.

He went back to his own childhood and that same school, when it was still a church and classes were kept everywhere

including the vestry. Sometimes six or eight of them would sit on a bench made for four. And he remembered Edith telling him about the school she went to before her parents moved to Woods: how they used to sit on bamboo benches, and how some parents, who thought their children were too good, used to bring their own little chairs with wooden frames and river rush seats, and how the others used to laugh.

They had remained community people in Birmingham. The West Indian community. Edith especially used to be asked to play for things at the infant and primary schools, and to bake for cake sales. He had noticed that these schools had a chair for every child. Perhaps he could adopt a class and make sure every child in it had a chair. These days, the corporations were adopting schools. Every day the newspaper mentioned another one. You bet none of them would come to adopt the school at Woods. There was no rule that said an individual couldn't. He wouldn't have to move about much. Most of his tools were electric. Woods had electricity and he had brought transformers.

'Edith?'

'Mhmm?'

'You can spare me a minute?'

'Coming.'

He put the idea to Edith.

'Capital!' she said.

He was surprised at her enthusiasm. He had expected support, but this was more than that. He couldn't know that she had been worrying about what the inactivity would do to him, worrying about living with somebody who was bored.

'You never can tell, you know. Somebody might be willing to give some lumber, and things like nails we can get at Mr Joseph's. I hear it still going strong. In fact, you could even start with the wood from the packing crates. Mass Zee could help you dismantle them. Some of that board is quite sturdy, but you going to have to plane it a lot.'

Edith sensed in herself a little something more than relief in his finding something to excite him: something more like pride in his having thought of such a project.

33

*   *   *

On Sunday, in the churchyard, Janet greeted them as usual
and said she was definitely coming to see them. Edith stopped
her sentence with, 'So is Christmas,' then told her to really
come by, because they wanted to talk with her about something.

People who had known them before had been trickling
in one by one to have a drink and a little chat. Not in any
planned way, but passing from their field, Maas Ize and Mass
Jerome, gentlemen who still wore old felt hats, would stop
and sit a while, talking over rum and water, resting their hats
on their knees. And David would drink his coconut water and
explain to them that that was the price he was paying for the
few more years the good Lord had granted him. The women
hardly came in the week. But on a Sunday afternoon, some
one or sometimes two would spend an hour or so.

Sometimes, the women brought their grandchildren, little
ones they were raising for their children who lived in town.
And Edith would think sometimes about the children they
never had and give thanks that David wasn't one of those
ignorant men who feel that, if you don't have children, you
are a mule. He always said that God gave them Laura, but
spared them the trouble of having to look after her when
she was little.

It was during these visits that invariably some name would
come up and they got to learn that So and So had died.
And some of the dead ones had been considerably younger
than they. So much to thank God for, David would say, and
apologize aloud for ever flying in God's face by complaining
because he was not one hundred per cent.

Janet came on Saturday, during the day, with a bottle of
ginger beer, and some jimbilins from a tree near her house
to see if David would remember how he used to steal them.
She was still living at the same house. Her father had died
but her mother was still alive, she said. Very old and blind,
but surprisingly cheerful. Perhaps they wouldn't recognize
the house, because over the years she had renovated and
changed it bit by bit.

She thought the bench and desk idea was a great one and insisted that God had sent them and the idea just at the right time. They so badly needed seating. Under her breath, she mumbled something about it being better to teach somebody to fish than to give them a fish. Aloud she asked if David would consider having her send some of the bigger boys so they could learn the trade from him and help make the benches and desks.

The more they talked, the more the project took shape. And it looked like it was going to be permanent, for what she suggested was that after they had used up what wood David could get, if he didn't mind he could start coming over to the school to supervise the repairing of those benches and desks that needed it. And that is how David virtually became the woodwork teacher for the school. And the boys were only too glad to be doing something that took them off the school premises and allowed them to steal people's oranges on the way down, without too much competition.

She had an idea for Edith, too. Not that she should really teach the bigger girls domestic science, just the finer things – how to set a table, how to eat with a knife and fork, how to make a bed and who knows what other little things she could help them with – call it "influence", but make it work like a sort of club so they would think of it not so much as lessons but as fun. It could meet once a week, but definitely not on the same day the boys came for woodwork, for that would be too taxing. 'Only taxing?' asked Edith. 'That would be looking for complication too, unless things change since my time.'

'Not a bit,' said Janet. 'You right.'

Edith would go along with the plan on one condition – that the girls would dress the church every Saturday. The way they used to do it when she was young. She said she wasn't at all satisfied with how it looked on Sundays. They went into a session remembering the fern-backed patterns they used to make over the altar when they were girls, and the red and yellow shoe blacks they used to put in there that couldn't last more than the day.

'Nobody calls them shoe black now,' Janet offered. 'Even I forget we used to call them that. Everybody saying Hibiscus.'

'Oh.'

'We will have to go and help the first few weeks till it gets off the ground.'

'Fine by me,' said Edith.

'I'm glad you are here, Edith. You know, I had forgotten how we used to dress church. Now is only for weddings and those are so rare in this church!'

Edith and Janet had been pupil teachers together in that same school. After college, she had not come back immediately but had taught in various parishes. She told Edith that she had returned home eventually when Teacher King died and the headship became vacant. She said it was God's action, because soon after that her father got down and her mother really appreciated her company and help.

Her mother's sight started to fail soon after that. But she was comfortable and had no regrets, for her mother wasn't even miserable. Edith didn't bother to ask her about marriage. She had gone around with the same Mico fellow for many years. She would check with David after to see if he remembered what had happened to that.

They were able to work up another little project. Janet said that the multidisciplinary approach was the best of the new-fangled things in education. She saw the sense and agreed with it. A few of the brighter students were to interview David and Edith, each one focusing on a different aspect of the foreign experience. They would put out a sort of journal.

A column in the *Gleaner* for rural news a few months later read under St Mary: "Community/School involvement – returning residents create a model".

David and Edith were doing the school a big favour, but they felt as if a big favour was being done to them. Leaving a district that had had so much going for it, and returning to find it so dead had been surprising and depressing. They had expected the district to move up in more than electric lights. In fact, it seemed to have moved down.

They hadn't discussed it with each other, but secretly each of them felt sort of responsible, almost as if they shouldn't have left, as if they had abandoned something that had needed all the help it could get to maintain itself. As if they were partly responsible for the decline. It wasn't a

reasonable feeling. People have to do what they feel is right for themselves sometimes. And they knew that. It felt right at the time, although the weeping and general sadness of everybody when they said they were going had hurt. Now they were wondering again.

People think of country districts as not having anything much going on. But Woods Village had never been like that. Every association that you can think of had a branch there back in the days before they left – Banana Growers, Cocoa Growers, Citizens' Association, Thrift Club. They had bought their organ from savings through the Thrift Club. And there had been a drama group. David had a flair for drama. In fact, he had written and produced a play one time in which both of them had leading rôles. It had something to do with migration, too – something about a father going to farm work in America, and promising to bring pretty clothes for his children, then absconding and never writing to his family to explain. There had been a club house then. Not a big exciting structure, but one built with community blood and sweat.

They had been shocked to see the structure when they returned. You could still read on marble squares around the base of what was left the names of those who had contributed to the building of the hall. But the roof was now no more than twisted sheets of metal, brown with rust. Irregular areas of surviving concrete marked where the walls had been. Apparently, several hurricanes, the most recent having been the most severe, had left their marks on it. Philosophical ideas about time and decay found easy examples in the remains of that building. Vast and trunkless legs of stone again.

Many a night, they had carried stones in the moonlight to mix mortar for the foundation. And many an evening had found him helping make wooden frames for the windows. He had already established himself as a carpenter then.

The land had been given by Mr Walker, the man whose shop had all along been used as a makeshift club house. Everybody in the district wanted to give something to what would be there for them and their children to use. Just remembering the moonlight nights with everybody out there

helping made Edith smile to herself. She could still put her hands on the photograph the man from the *Welfare Reporter* had taken when the Member of Parliament for the area had come for the opening. She would take it to Kingston and make them enlarge it. She wasn't sure why.

The building had served as club house in the night and Basic School during the day – a blessing to parents of small children they didn't know what to do with. It had been a good time. Government was just getting interested in doing something for people under seven years old (which was the age at which they could go to "big school"). The children got a hot lunch, usually cornmeal porridge and some sort of whole wheat bun. What had happened to all of that?

Once a month, it was a cinema, too. The man with the Delco generator would come and, for a small fee, show a movie to a full house. And on public holidays, there would always be a sound-system dance.

Now she could stay on her hilltop and see, at all hours of the day, children under seven holding on to their mothers' frock tails going to the stand pipe for water or going for the water by themselves, carrying white plastic bottles they could barely manage. She found herself feeling sorry for them and then wondered if she was becoming a tourist, always sorry for the locals. For didn't she herself at those ages carry at least the water that was used to bathe her? No, she wasn't worried about the water carrying, but about the time of day and what they should be doing instead.

It was easy to feel that a whole part of the nation would be left behind forever if, when children of their age in other parts of the country were going to school, they were either carrying water themselves or going with their mothers to get it. She might have to take that on, too. She wouldn't do it herself, though. Must be able to find somebody who could. Must be able to write a petition to some agency and get help. Only if everything failed would she offer to pay the salary. A slice out of the rent from the townhouse might do that. If, for a few cents, you could save part of a generation, what's the odds, she was thinking.

* * *

People from Rock Spring and Dry Land were saying that Woods Village had gone to sleep, and that Mass David and Miss Edith had come back to wake it up. They said they were waiting on their own awakening, but had no idea who would do it. But that was not the full story. A few other things happened around the same time to make it seem so. Especially the repairing of the road.

Governments had come and gone over the years, and it didn't matter which party was in power, nobody ever fixed the road to Woods Village. You might say that the days of Banana were over in the district, and there was no interest in getting a product for export out to the bay. Or you might say, no member of parliament nor his mother lived in the district. If you hadn't been watching long enough, you would even say that the people supported the wrong party. All parties had been wrong for Woods Village then.

One bright day, contractors appeared out of nowhere, hiring people to work on the road. Then men came with pressers, rolling back and forth to smooth the rough stones, and set up cauldrons of steaming tar. In no time, the road was paved. And you didn't have to worry about your car anymore and, better than anything else, the minibus drivers started to say that, for a dollar more, they would drive that extra mile in from Palmetto. Nobody explained why this happened. Of course, there were rumours not to be repeated. People spoke about them with their fingers curved over their lips.

But if after all this time the village suddenly found favour with some politician for whatever reason, who was to question it? Everybody simply said Thank God and whispered about moral issues.

In a poor district, money is like leaven: a little goes a long way. Before David and Edith got their own crops going, they were buying fruit and vegetables from different people. There were items they needed that Mass Freddie started to stock in his shop, things that nobody had been buying there before. Items like tissues, which had replaced the handkerchief, and dishwashing fluid, were part of their new life. People passing through and going into the bowels of St Mary, public servants going about their business, got to know you could buy certain things there. And when

the road was no longer a threat, more traffic was willing to pass.

Young people working in town or down at Bay, whose parents still lived in Woods and its surroundings, started coming home more frequently to visit their parents and the children they were invariably raising for them. Even Church got a little lift in attendance. All in all, the district was getting busy.

Chapter V   New life

Life started to take on a certain definite shape for David and Edith. They were busy, but not overworked. Edith had forgotten what it was like to have somebody to help in the house. It is true that in Birmingham the house had been carpeted, and the air was never dry and full of dust. Even so, there was always the washing and the vacuuming to be done somewhere between the hospital run and the music lessons. Soon after they arrived back in Woods, Mabel had come by to see them. She was the granddaughter of Miss Evvy who used to work for them before they left, and she wanted to know if they needed anybody. She hadn't done domestic work before. She had graduated from Vocational School. She hadn't had a chance to look for a job. Almost as soon as she graduated, she found herself in the family way (they hadn't heard it described like that in a long time – clearly she couldn't be blamed for a condition in which she "found herself"). The children were all going to school and she wanted to look out for herself.

They heard her story, marvelling all the while at the youthful look on her face in spite of all her woes. She didn't plan on having any more children. The boyfriend she had, who wasn't the children's father, worked in town, and whenever he came up, they took precaution. She was older, she said, and meant wiser.

Mabel came every day by eight o'clock in time to make them a good breakfast. They would sit down and enjoy boiled banana and mackerel, or ackee and saltfish, or calaloo and fried dumpling, and when she really felt energetic, hominy corn porridge, which was a great favourite with both of them.

Who ever heard of breakfast in Birmingham? You grabbed your cup of coffee, scalded your lips and rushed out the door, and the first time you really sat down to eat was tea and a scone at nine-thirty. By the time it came, it was a king's meal, you were so hungry.

They had a light lunch – sandwich and a drink – and

whenever Mabel finished cooking the dinner and doing whatever else she had to do, she could go. Two days a week, she was supposed to serve lemonade to the school children who came for their woodwork or their influence, but that was it. Edith figured it was meet and right that her helper's children shouldn't have to come home to an empty house just because their mother was earning.

From time to time, Edith would remember her friends. Other black women who were to weather the cold until arthritis forced them to take it no more. Her secret fear had been to trip on a wet pavement and break her hip. There but for the grace . . . talk about being unfeignedly thankful. She even had time to read now.

* * *

As soon as the road was fixed, Janet wrote to the public library to say the Bookmobile could start to service the district. Every Thursday, it went over to the school and came down the hill to come to a stop at Rose Level, which is the first flat spot you reach as you drive away from the school. A path led from there into a maze of districts that were suburbs, so to speak, of Woods. And it was just in front of David and Edith's castle. And that is how they started taking library books again.

The first night, Edith found a joke in a book she was reading and called to David to share it. He listened and laughed, and "Read to the end of the scene for me now". They kept on laughing long after the joke had disappeared. They must have laughed quite loudly, because a young man passing on the road shouted, "Go deh!!"

Who could understand why two people over sixty were laughing like school children? In the days before England, when they were still using "Home Sweet Home" lamps, this reading to each other had been their chief pastime. In those days, the package of books came by mail from Port Maria once a week, and the set you were returning passed the set you were receiving in the postman's bag somewhere. You would request books, but you were never sure that you would get what you requested. You might have to settle for the librarian's choice if she didn't have what you wanted. These were home delivered and self selected at your very door. What a privilege!!

You would have thought it couldn't ever come to this again. You would have thought they had lost the ability to read together. The truth is that what they used to read in Birmingham was the newspaper and little else. Nothing had replaced the recreational reading to each other that had been a part of their early living together. You might have thought the cinema in England would have taken its place. Somehow, it hadn't. Perhaps the rain and cold had prevented them from developing the habit. And so, with an ease that shocked even themselves, they fell back into this communal reading habit with the occasional mug of cocoa to warm the stomach.

The reverberating ring of their laughter marked the beginning of the whole of that.

* * *

People who have no experience of plants find it difficult to understand how quickly things grow. In six months, there were lively vines in discreet patches about the yard. There was callalloo already cut with a few stalks seeding to be planted again, and there were tomato plants with small green and yellow flowers about to become fruit.

The yard was beautiful. Mass Zee was obviously an artist. The hedge was thick and neatly cut with the occasional touch of pink and red hibiscus peeping out. There was a mango tree in the front yard, laden with cho chos. That was David's idea. The mango tree had so many leaves he swore it would never bear fruit, so he trained the cho cho vines onto it. It was white cho cho. People said it was good for high blood pressure. Edith's pressure sometimes acted up, so he decided to plant that variety. Cho cho was easy to grow, especially in a rainy place like Woods.

David was making a point of planting the vegetables Edith liked. A part of him remembered how she used to quarrel in the before-England days about having to buy vegetables when her husband was a farmer. In those days, he was concentrating on big crops, especially bananas. Those that could bring in a lump sum. Her argument then was that if they saved some pennies off small things like tomatoes, some pounds would get taken care of. In defiance she had planted her own little bed behind the kitchen. Now that

he had no big crops, he found it easy to concentrate on vegetables. He really wanted to please her. He told himself that most people didn't get a second chance and he was one of the lucky ones.

*   *   *

Laura's surprise bordered on shock when she visited her uncle and aunt no more than six months after she had settled them in. She had visited once before, but that was the week after she took them down. Shortly after, she had gone off to a course in London, courtesy of the office. She had taken the opportunity to go down to Birmingham as much to visit some of her old friends as to see some of theirs who she had come to know during the years at the centre. Everyone was interested and hungry for news of them, as if they were guinea pigs or a pilot project everyone else was looking to. She had brought a few gifts and a lot of news. They belonged to a generation that was yearning, every last one of them, to return home. To be buried under their own vine and fig tree, they liked to say.

She went down on a Saturday to allow herself the luxury of spending the weekend. She had sent a telegram to say she was coming. That was really more ritual than necessity. In any case, she wouldn't have been surprised if the telegram arrived after she had come and gone. The hedge, as neat as a well-coiffed afro, was visible as soon as she took the curve at Rose Level. There was a discreet sign on the gate saying "Edaville". She smiled, and made up her mind to remember to put that on the envelope the next time she wrote them. It would look good and they would feel good. The mango-cho cho tree came into view. That cracked her up. What were they trying to do?

She was further impressed when she saw what was called the guest room, but was really her room. There were two beds in there. Made by hand. Four lengths of mahoe nailed together with slats across the breadth and a foam mattress fitted in made one. The fact that there were two was a signal that she could bring a friend. It also allowed them to have couples visit and stay over. Who knows, they might even be

thinking of starting up bridge again. They used to tell her about the all-night bridge sessions of their youth.

The room had a finished look. It appeared carpeted because the rug, brought from the house in England, filled up all the visible parts of it. There was a desk, too, of the same mahoe, and open shelves against the wall. A full-length mirror was attached to one wall, but there was no place for hanging clothes. Obviously, guests were expected to wear T-shirts and jeans.

One bed had a plain calico sheet, but the other had a patchwork spread of the most delicate colours, patterned brown and beige with a touch of blue close to the colour of the rug.

'That is your aunt's handiwork, my dear,' David said, as he noticed the surprise on Laura's face. 'It's her latest pastime. Every evening, she stitch until night fall. Say she doing it by natural light.'

'Talk about me?' said Edith, coming along the corridor. 'Is him build the bed and the desk and all the furniture in there, you hear, Laura, hammering day and night.'

'If I close my eyes, I will become a pumpkin,' Laura said, and hugged them tightly in turn.

What Laura didn't talk about was the agility with which her uncle was moving. She thought he might be self-conscious if she commented. But she couldn't help saying as she gazed at her aunt's face, 'What a way the two of you look well.' She couldn't get over the relaxed look, such a far cry from the tightness she had noted that day that seemed so long ago when she met them at Norman Manley airport. She was thinking that she had her own hotel now for any time the city got too much for her.

'You don't know what you have done,' she said. 'You will soon get tired of seeing me.'

'Never,' they said, as if they had rehearsed the response.

She reported on the friends in Birmingham. Especially those who had made a start in the trying to come home. Three or four of them had bought into the same housing scheme outside of Spanish Town, and were waiting for the houses to be built and water and light to be put in. The dates kept getting pushed further and further, and the price kept escalating.

45

David's illness had frightened them all into worrying about making it home alive. None of these people came from places they wanted to go back to. They had sold what little they had to find the fare to go to England. David and Edith had been lucky. They had been in a different situation. They hadn't sold their house. They had never thought of England as anything but an opportunity to make some money. Certainly not a place to settle in forever.

Sunday after dinner, Laura said she had a suggestion to make. She warned them that it was a selfish suggestion, no matter how unselfish it sounded. She wanted them to celebrate their having been home for a year with a get-together. It would be for their friends, those they could find, but she should be allowed to invite her friends and as many cousins as she could locate, certainly those in Kingston. They thought it was a good idea. She wanted it in October, although that would be a little beyond the year.

'But Laura,' her uncle asked, 'October no the rainiest month of the year?'

'Well . . . but isn't it in the last part that the rain falls?'

'No, mam. All parts. You see, you always used to come here in holidays, so you don't know anything after August. Ask anybody.'

'Let me put it this way, Uncle D. If government can bet on October, I can.'

'What government have to do with it?'

'Well, they decide to hold back a piece of the festival celebration and have it during Heritage Week. You know, the National Heroes weekend.'

'You forget that we don't know anything about all that.'

'OK. You know at least that Independence celebrations are in August.'

'Mhm.'

'Well, they have all kinds of competition connected with it. Schools and communities are involved. They have the Parish Finals and eventually the Island Finals in Kingston. I am always interested in the traditional dance section. I don't think Woods has been participating, but I know for sure other St Mary communities have been. I mean, when you

say St Mary out in the wide Jamaica, anybody who knows anything about culture will say "Dinkimini".'

'Say what?' David shouted characteristically. 'I haven't seen that since Maas Isaac died. I must have been about nine. Edith, you wouldn't remember, because you didn't live around here yet. Manalva in there too, Laura? The one with king and queen?'

'I think that is what they call Bruckins now, you know, but I am not sure. Bruckins has king and queen and sword. That might be it. But you will see for yourself and you can tell me. I would like us to have this get-together the day before Mento Yard, which is what they call it now. It's really a big fair with a lot of music. They keep it in Lawrence Park in St Ann's Bay, which is not really so far from here. I will sleep over and we all can drive there. You will get a chance to see the whole thing. They have food from all parts of the island. Things I am sure you forget exist. Last year, I had colic for days, I had mixed up so many different things in my stomach.'

'You think two old people can manage that?' Edith asked. 'One day party and the other day fair?'

Laura laughed. 'The old people I see here can manage more than that.'

'If you say so, my lady.'

'Alright, that's a deal. I have to go to travel late July, I think . . .'

'But what a way you always travelling?'

'I notice you never said a thing about it when you were in England and I used to pass through so often. That time, it suited you, eh?'

'Is true,' Edith said, and they all laughed.

'Anyway, you are right. Even I am getting a little tired of it now. We can do the planning when I get back. That will give me an excuse to be down here most weekends, as if I needed one. You can start thinking about it, though, and when I come back down, we can have full-scale discussions about the guest list and food. I just wanted to be sure you go along with the idea.'

'That sounds like more than enough time. And it certainly is a very good idea. I can see Charley and Myrtle down here already,' David said.

PART II

Chapter VI   Brenda

Standing in the line for single luggage only, Laura heard a commotion. Two lines away, a young black woman was stringing together words that were entirely unsuitable for that location. Unsuitable, in fact, anywhere. She was telling the customs officer about parts of the anatomy he couldn't possibly possess. She was swinging her head fiercely from side to side, so that the narrow lengths of plait were moving like long rat tails in and out of her eyes. Two large suitcases were open on the examination table with their guts askew. The officer had dared to open the suitcases and, what was more, he had dared not to open those of the passenger ahead of her. The other passenger was white.

A brand new blender, an iron and something that looked like a transformer were on top of the table. Price tags were still apparent on some of them. A video camera with its case beside it was also on the table. The officer was saying that the declaration form had "Personal effects only" on it, and the young woman was telling him what a dunce he was not to know that those *were* personal effects. He wasn't answering her much. Giving her the quiet treatment which was like a match to her canefield.

Laura recognized the girl as being Brenda Smith, someone she had known in Birmingham several years before. She had spoken briefly to her in the waiting room at Heathrow and had been introduced to two arty looking young men she was playing cards with. SHE was coming home on some assignment or other and, she added *sotto voce*, to find her Jamaican self. THEY were going to Montego Bay to satisfy a long time dream and to be around for Reggae Sunsplash.

The young men had stayed on while they disembarked. Like most of the other passengers, they were going on to Montego Bay. The immigration line had gone quickly, but even with so few passengers, Customs had been slow.

Laura moved up in her own line. The shouting seemed to have died down. She allowed herself to relax.

'Laura!' It was Brenda's voice. The tone was only slightly less aggressive than when she addressed the officer. 'When you go outside, tell Gerald these damn people holding me up in here. You know him, don't you?'

'Yes, and I'll tell him.' Laura tried to look concerned.

However, by the time she got outside, Brenda was right behind her. Apparently, the customs officer had kept one suitcase and she would have to turn up at the Queen's Warehouse to claim it and pay duty on some of the things she had brought. Laura recognized Gerald. He had become somewhat of a celebrity in the world of theatre.

'Fix me up no', brother!' the porter said to him as he took a suitcase off his trolley.

'Don't give him a red cent.' That was Brenda, coming up behind the porter. 'People here don't know that you shouldn't get paid twice to do your job.'

Laura thought she remembered that porters expected tips wherever she had seen them, even if they were scarcer in England than in the US. But she said nothing. Without a word, Gerald ignored the command and handed a five-dollar bill to the man who paused in his expletives to say, 'Thanks'.

'We taking a van,' Gerald said. 'Somebody coming for you, Laura?'

'No,' she said, silently cursing the agreement she had come to with her friends that they wouldn't meet each other at the airport, but would travel with Jamaican dollars and allow those at home to find better use for their time.

'We can share the van, then.'

'OK.'

It was still light when the JUTA van moved out onto the Palisadoes road. The mountains were there on their side, as usual, touching the sky. And, as usual, Laura was marvelling at them. She had gone off into her reverie and forgotten the company. 'Every time I come home, I expect the mountains to have altered a bit, to have deteriorated just a little bit . . .'

Nobody commented. Brenda was obviously nursing her anger. Gerald was obviously respecting it.

Out onto the Rockfort Road, past the cement factory and on to Windward road, where the traffic started to back up

and forced the van to stop too long at a few spots one would rather not focus on. Brenda exploded.

'This damn country so nasty!' she said. 'The money they spend to pay people to search up people things they might use to clean up the streets.'

Laura wanted to say she hadn't thought of such an exchange, but decided against it. She had to admit that the street looked untidy. She tried to see it all through Brenda's eyes. They were both coming from a cleaner place. She had overnighted in London coming through from Stockholm. Scandinavian cities are notoriously clean. One evening in London, she had gone walking and had noted the extraordinary health of the roses, in colours hardly hoped for – deep red, orange, purple in the front garden of all but the uninhabited houses. And there was no uncared-for garbage anywhere.

All along the road from the airport, there were makeshift provision stalls on the ground, each with its stack of garbage near it. There were more flies there than one expected. Laura remembered how, long ago, one of her cousins had remarked that the entry to Kingston was always dirty and unwelcoming. He had been living in New York then. Not a particularly clean city, but hardly dingy. At least, not where they used to live. He admitted, though, that it made the clean part as you whisked along Mountain View Avenue into Old Hope Road look good by comparison.

Listening to Brenda, Laura started to think about perspective and how people interpret phenomena depending on the lenses they wear. Everything got on Brenda's nerves. First the driving. She couldn't understand how the driver could allow people to cut in ahead of him after passing him on the wrong side. Immediately afterwards, she couldn't understand how he could do the same thing.

'I will never drive in this country,' she said.

'Calm down no', Brenda,' Gerald said, 'me not driving neither, but for a different reason. Me can't buy car.' He gave a mirthless laugh in which nobody joined.

The stadium came into view. It was almost time for them to get off. Gerald talked to the driver and gave him their share of the money.

'Brenda, you must call me when you settle down,' Laura said, as the vehicle came to a halt.

'How long you say you have again?'

'About three months.'

Laura handed her the card the office provided, all the while feeling sure that it wouldn't be used. She was accustomed to being considered square by the Brendas of this world. She didn't expect her to call unless, of course, there was some service she could provide. Laura always expected a certain amount of pragmatism from people. She hoped she wasn't being unfair.

She remembered Brenda as different and a little sad, but the aggressiveness and the strong negative reaction to Jamaica, those were new. Something must have happened to sour her so. She wondered just how often she had returned home, but she couldn't ask her anything on the way. Her mood was too foul.

Chapter VII Brenda retrospective

Brenda had left Jamaica when she was fourteen. In the third form. She had been looking forward to leaving for a whole year. The week of her common entrance results, her mother had told her that her father said he would like to take over her education. When she was in second form, her mother told her that he had filed for her. It would probably take a year or more. She felt a little sad that she was leaving her mother and her grandmother, but she felt privileged to be going up. Third form year felt unreal. She was there but, she knew that at any time she might not be there. She was waiting on the visa to come through. She knew other children who were waiting on the same thing. They weren't bothering with their school work because they were going to America. She couldn't try that. 'It can't do you any harm to take a good report with you up there,' her mother had said, and continued to supervise her homework.

Everybody considered her lucky when the visa came through in only a year. Her father had been in New York then. She ended up in London several years later, when her father married a Jamaican nurse who he met when she visited her sister in America.

The traffic usually goes in the other direction – England to the USA. Especially with nurses. But this one was warned by her sister, who had made that journey, that night duty for days on end is what the Americans have waiting for black nurses coming from England. But she said the salary was good. Not good enough, though, for a woman with neither chick nor child. She liked her sleep time. Besides, she had grown to like England and the cheap fares to the continent, which were easy to come by when she needed a break. Brenda knew the story by heart.

That first year in America remained indelible in her mind. She wasn't sure what she had expected. She knew it wasn't what she got. From that first Saturday afternoon when she landed, full of dreams, she knew they were just that – dreams.

Not that she had any choice. She would have had to go to her father whether she wanted to or not. But she had wanted to. Everybody wanted to go to the States.

Ivan Smith was living with an Afro-American woman then. Brenda never figured out what had caused him to decide to send for her. The woman had a daughter about her own age, but age was all they had in common. She got the feeling the day after she landed that they all thought she was there to be the maid.

Brenda did not know her father. She had seen him a few times when he had come to visit them in Jamaica, and had enjoyed the feeling of elation a child gets when a parent from abroad is visiting. He always left her with an American note, ten or twenty dollars, for which the bank would give her more Jamaican money for her savings book than she put in at one time, even when she stayed with Mrs King's children every Saturday for a whole term.

Brenda did not know her father. She wanted to get to know him. She wanted to make him her friend. She had invested a lot of imagination in what her life with him would be like. She had not spent any time thinking about a stepmother. She was soon to discover that neither Johnnie, the stepmother, nor Lyn, her daughter, was happy to have her. Johnnie had not been part of the decision to bring her partner's child to America. She had been presented with the fact. At one point, Brenda decided her father had looked at the situation and saw he wasn't getting anything out of it because he had no children there. That's why he had sent for her. But she would never know if that was the reason.

True to everything the story books say, Johnnie regarded Brenda as competition, especially for her gentleman's money. When he used to send money for her in Jamaica, it was never more than fifty dollars, and that not on a regular basis. She knew, because she used to buy the money orders. In New York, that couldn't even feed her. Lyn and herself would suffer, no matter how indirectly, for this addition. She would need pocket money and clothes, and the man was not getting a raise of pay. He wasn't looking for a second job, either, as far as she could see.

Brenda needed a buffer against day-to-day antagonism. But her father didn't provide it. He didn't seem to be aware of any but her physical needs. He wouldn't make the time to talk with her and she never understood why. His time with her was always mixed up with his time with Johnnie or with Johnnie and Lyn. Years later, when she tried to find reasons, she wondered whether the ability to relate to your children is a learned thing and he just had not had any opportunity to learn.

Brenda felt that there was a conspiracy against her mother. Nobody said so. But she felt it. Take the day she connected up the blender parts with the rubber on the wrong side: 'Yaawl don't have this in your house in Jamaica?' Brenda had chosen to regard it as a rhetorical question and had said nothing.

Or the day her father's church shirt had a crease in it: 'You mother ain't teach you to iron shirt?'

This Brenda regarded as another rhetorical question. In fact, she had wondered whether her father used to wear his shirts rough dry to church before she came. But she didn't dare ask. Johnnie had already told her father she was insolent. She had heard that by being in the wrong place at the right time. She knew that silence always meant insolence, to adults.

She didn't think her mother's name had any place in this woman's mouth. *She* didn't know her mother. *She* didn't know anything about her. Nor would she ever know what a single woman supporting herself and a child on a cashier's job in Kingston is all about. Especially when the child's father only sends money when he feels like it.

Brenda never ever forgave Johnnie. Years later, when she was working in England and had done well enough to help her own mother buy a small townhouse in Kingston, she found herself hoping that Lyn had not been able to do any such thing for Johnnie.

The clothes were another problem. Nearly anything she put on met with Lyn's disapproval.

'Nobody ain't wearing that here.'

She seemed to hear that whether she dressed for church or for the occasional Saturday afternoon cinema. She was

relieved when her father bought her two pairs of jeans and a pair of Reeboks. That took a great weight off her. With a T-shirt and those, she could feel comfortable on a Saturday.

Church remained a problem for a long time. Especially when the winter came. Miss Ruby, her mother's dressmaker and friend from schooldays, had made two linen dresses out of material her mother could hardly afford. She didn't feel cold in them because her coat was warm. But there seemed to be some unwritten rule against linen when it was winter, and neither she, nor her mother, nor Miss Ruby had been told about it. If Miss Ruby knew, she wouldn't have made the dresses. She would have made church ones for her mother instead. She wouldn't want her to look bad. Miss Ruby used to go up to New York often, so Brenda never understood how she didn't find out about that.

Only in retrospect did Brenda work out that jealousy might have been part of the problem between herself and Lyn. Lyn was Brenda's height, but fifty pounds heavier. No wonder. At every meal, she ate more than Brenda and her mother between them ate in one day at home. And the cooking was different from what she was accustomed to. Everything was fried, and every meal was washed down with large amounts of soft drink called soda.

Whenever a holiday was coming up, Lyn would say, 'I'm going on a diet.' Johnnie didn't seem to mind either, although she herself was a small woman.

School was the other problem. Her mother had made it clear to her that she had to get a good education in America. She didn't want to disappoint her mother. And every time things didn't go her way, she told herself it was for her own good so she could get the education that her mother couldn't afford to give her. Apparently, if she went to high school in America, she would be able to go to college there. At least, that is what her father must have told her mother. But there was so much that she didn't understand. She had been a bright child at home. She hadn't come lower than fourth in the form in her three years in high school. She had hoped to keep that up, but it looked impossible.

She spent the first week, or so it seemed to her, taking various tests in the office of the counsellor who wanted to

know every thing about her life, from how many grand-mothers she had alive to how she felt about her stepmother. She thought she had understood her mother to have said that a good report was all she needed to get into school in America. Maybe her mother didn't know about Placement Tests and Diagnostic Tests. And the counsellor said she could make no sense of the reports from home.

Eventually, she was placed in a Grade Nine class where everybody seemed to have known everybody else from Grade One. Every day, she had to miss classes to go downstairs to a "home room" where she was sent to be with other West Indian children in the school. This was supposed to be good for her psychologically. It was very bad for her in terms of her plans for herself. She was supposed to feel at home for that brief period. But she didn't feel at home. She simply felt that she had missed classes that might be important.

Only two of the children in the home room were from Jamaica – Jenny and herself. She found herself spending her time teaching Jenny to read. Jenny was eleven and very slow. She said she had gone to school in Jamaica, but she must have sat in the back row all her years or been absent most of the time, she knew so little. She could hardly read and spoke patwa all the time. The teacher smiled when Jenny spoke, but Brenda was sure she didn't understand anything Jenny said. And Jenny certainly didn't understand anything the teacher said.

There were boys and girls of all ages from all territories of the Caribbean in that home room. Sean was from Trinidad and Jeff from Grand Cayman. She wouldn't forget those two. They were always up to mischief. It was easy to spend your time playing box and tee taa toe when nothing that was going on made any sense.

There was a strange girl there. From Guyana. She was very pretty. She was older than the rest of them and kept talking about Kamgee. She didn't always sound lucid, and the teacher couldn't find out whether Kamgee was person, place or thing. Brenda couldn't understand why a big girl like that was at school, not work. Months later, she was told that in America you had the legal right to stay in school till you were nineteen. Everything there was either legal or illegal.

They were supposed to get to know each other and to enjoy a feeling of being at home, since they were all from the same place. Two college students came every day to help them with school work and with any simple adjustment problems. But they were all from such different grades and backgrounds the thing was impossible. The teacher in charge of the class was from Haiti. She had a good heart, but she had not spoken to many people from the anglophone islands before she took that job. There were no Haitians in the class. She liked the children, but could not help them. They had hired her because she was from the Caribbean. She was one of the children's people. It was the kind of normal suggestion that allows foreigners to expect Jamaicans to play steel band and Trinidadians to play reggae music, as if the region were one large homogenous mass.

Brenda was lucky to have gone to a school where teachers were from all over the Caribbean. She had grown accustomed to strange accents. She understood what the Haitian teacher said, and what all the students said, as long as they were talking about something she was familiar with. She was always being called upon to translate.

Of course, American was different from all the Caribbean accents, and she had a harder time in the regular classes. Seemed as if all the teachers were talking from far up in their nose. But as long as she concentrated, she could understand. And if she spoke slowly, even those teachers seemed to understand her.

One morning, a Jamaican woman visited the school and came to talk to the home room class. Brenda didn't know she was so homesick. She was so glad to hear the woman's voice she felt she was going to cry. The woman said her name was Mrs Saul. She was from Jamaica, but she knew about the other islands. She had even lived in some of them. She talked to each of them, including the older girl, and told everybody that Canje was a place in Guyana. She put up a map of the Caribbean on the wall and said it was her gift to them. She gave each person a small paper heart. They were to write their names on the hearts and she helped stick them on the map near the countries they came from. She made

each of them stand and tell the class something about their country. She told them to try to remember where the persons sitting on either side of them came from. The Haitian teacher thanked her and thanked her, and made each of them say thanks in their own words. Brenda had been sitting in the corner. She was the last to speak., She stood up and was barely able to say thank you. Her voice was shaking.

Mrs Saul came across and hugged her. She looked at the teacher. The teacher nodded and she took Brenda outside. It was the fall. They went to sit on a bench under a tree whose leaves were all yellow and purple. Brenda's eyes took that in. It looked a little like a star-apple tree, but she knew it was not. She was in America. Mrs Saul told her she should cry if she wanted to. But she didn't cry.

'Brenda, you're ready to tell me what's wrong?' Mrs Saul's arm was around her shoulders. She couldn't answer. Her throat was tight. Like when she went to tell her Granny goodbye and the old lady said that she didn't think she would see her again. That's the way her throat felt then.

Mrs Saul waited. She didn't seem to be in a hurry. They were alone under the tree. Suddenly, Brenda began to cry. Then she stopped. But great sobs continued to shake her body. Mrs Saul was rocking her gently, the way you would hush a small child.

'You don't have to be afraid to tell me anything. I won't tell anybody. In any case, I am going back to Jamaica tomorrow. Don't keep it in. That only makes it worse. Just talk. You will feel better.'

For some reason, Brenda felt she could trust her. She told her the truth. She wasn't doing well in the regular class. She was wasting time with the group in the home room. Nobody was helping her down there. All she was doing was helping Jenny because she was sorry for her. She was afraid of turning dunce. She didn't want to be put in a remedial class, where one of the mainstream teachers said she would go if her grades didn't improve. The teacher had already sent the other black girl in her class there. Mrs Saul said she wasn't promising anything, but she would speak to the students who were helping with the class and ask them to pay some attention to her. She would speak with the class teacher, too.

She asked about home. Brenda went silent again. Eventually she spoke. She said it was terrible. Then the whole story about Johnnie and Lyn and her father came out. Mrs Saul asked her where her father worked. She mentioned the Jamaican bakery. Mrs Saul's forehead creased and her eyes looked intent. She asked her if that was the same as Stewart's bakery. It was.

It didn't matter to Brenda that Mrs Saul couldn't do anything for her. She felt much better for having talked. Somebody had listened to her. That was more than anyone had done since she reached America. She even offered to take a letter for her mother. She decided to write the letter and to buy a magazine at the drugstore on her way home. She had five dollars in her pocket. Her mother liked to read *Essence*. Mrs Saul would stop by for the letter next day on her way to the airport.

Things started to fall into place. Brenda spent less and less time in the home room and she got the occasional "Good work" on her book in some of the subjects in the regular class. Mrs Saul wrote to her, care of the home room teacher. She was very surprised. She said Brenda should write to her whenever she felt she needed to talk to somebody.

By November, the place had become quite cold. Not inside. That was always very warm. But even the walk to the school bus stop, just a few blocks away, was trying. People tell you about the cold, but it is difficult to understand it till you feel it yourself. Just so people had told her about the subway. But again, the notion of walking down into the bowels of the earth and finding a whole world of trains down there was difficult to come to terms with.

March came. It was harsh, the way every poem she had read described it. She felt she couldn't take it any longer. One of the girls in church told her that by April everything would be fine again. She told her that she would soon get accustomed to it and even prefer it to the heat of June and July.

'You wish,' said Brenda, and sighed out loud.

Chapter VIII   Help

One Saturday in May, Ivan telephoned from work. Johnnie spoke to him and gave Brenda an envelope to take to him at the bakery. When she got there, he took the envelope and asked Brenda if she had eaten. She hadn't, so he said she should go over to the restaurant attached to the bakery and wait. She didn't have to wait long. He came, and without asking her what she wanted, ordered a patty and a glass of ginger beer for her and a bottle of Red Stripe for himself. She hadn't eaten a patty since she left home. It was the first time she had visited her father's workplace. She didn't even know that they made patties there. He never brought patties home. He brought a hardough loaf home every Saturday, and at Easter he had brought home a huge bun. But that was all. She noticed that there were all sorts of things she liked to eat there. Potato pudding, gizada, coconut drops. She had enough money in her purse. She would buy two gizadas to take home.

Ivan finished his beer and left. He told her she should eat the lunch and wait on him. Brenda finished the ginger beer in one long guzzle. She hardly noticed how strong it was. Her lips and throat started to tingle as soon as she finished. They had served her the patty with a fork. She stuck the fork into the patty. She was struggling with it. The pieces that came off were only pastry. She wasn't reaching the meat in the centre. She had never eaten a patty with a fork. At home, she would hold the patty in its bag like everybody else and bite off a good chunk at a time.

A tall woman in a sweatsuit and Nike shoes with a whistle in her waist walked over to her.

'Take it up with your hand and eat it, my dear. Not a thing is wrong with that.'

Funny how her heart leapt when she heard a Jamaican woman talk. Same thing had happened when she had heard Mrs Saul. She looked up and smiled.

'Thank you,' she said, and picked up the patty.

'I am Joy Stewart.'

'Oh, I'm glad to meet you. I am Brenda Smith. My father works in the bakery. His name is Ivan Smith.'

'I know,' Mrs Stewart said, a kind of conspiratorial smile enveloping her face. 'And I know your grandmother. I used to buy ortaniques from her at home.'

'You are from down Porus way?' Brenda asked.

'Yes. I was born there, and when I was a little girl your grandmother used to give me grater cake and watch to see if I was stealing any of the guavas by the gate.' Brenda started to laugh. It meant this woman really knew her grandmother. She certainly had not laughed like that since she came to America. It was a laugh full of memory. Mrs Stewart had been responsible for getting her father legal in America.

Brenda put two and two together, and realized for the first time that her father had lived in the same district as her mother and grandmother. Her mother had never said much about him. Almost as if he was an event she wanted to forget.

They talked and talked for a long time. Mrs Stewart asked her about her school work and Brenda told her the truth. It was better than it had been when she first came, but she didn't feel confident, and when the new year started, she would have to go from Junior High to High School.

Mrs Stewart confessed that Mrs Saul had written to her.

'So you know her!' Brenda exclaimed.

'We were in school together a long time ago. In Jamaica.'

'Wow!' Brenda said.

Mrs Stewart wanted her to come over to the bakery every evening after school and on Saturdays. She wanted her to help her in the office and she would get three dollars an hour. Brenda did a quick calculation and saw at least twenty dollars a week in her hands.

'I'll have to ask my father.'

The slow smile that now seemed characteristic was enveloping Mrs Stewart's face again.

'That's OK,' she said. 'I have talked to him already. Come with me and let me show you the office.'

That Saturday was a turning point in Brenda's life.

During the summer, when the job was full-time, Mrs Stewart

looked at her school report and said, 'Brenda, a bright girl like you will have to get an A in English. I'm sure Joan won't mind helping you.'

Joan was the daughter of the Stewart household and was finishing a degree in Journalism at Columbia. Soft spoken and with a broad smile, she was a younger, shorter version of her mother. Of course she would help, she said, and suggested they work on American history as well.

The lessons were really quite painless. For the English, Joan would give her a theme to write on, then go over the work with her, suggesting how they could improve it. She would then do a rewrite. Later, they started discussing the topics first, then writing. She seldom had to rewrite.

Every week, Brenda would read a chapter of American history and Joan would set her some questions on the chapter and go over her answers with her.

It didn't take long for Mrs Stewart to find out that Brenda had a clothes problem. She told her she could wear her T-shirt and jeans on the job, and if Brenda didn't mind, she could select some good things from among those Joan didn't wear anymore. Brenda did not mind. Joan was about her height. Their figures were quite different, but they could fit into the same clothes. Brenda had shoulders. Joan had bosom. One could say the area was the same. There was a cupboard full of skirts and dresses that Joan, then in her twenties, wouldn't wear again. And they were sensible clothes, not affected too much by any changes in style.

At home, Lyn and her mother had a lot to say. Lyn announced that she could never wear anybody else's clothes. Johnnie said she was lucky that she could fit into other people's things. Brenda bit her lip and said nothing.

When the new school year started, Brenda entered Tenth Grade. She felt confident about her work. And she behaved as if she was no longer afraid of her own shadow, the way she used to be in Junior High. She had been Mrs Stewart's right-hand woman the whole summer. She had benefited from exposure to the Stewart household in many ways. Even in her speech. Everybody in that house spoke Jamaica patwa when they felt like it. Nobody there told her that she talked "funny". That was a remark she heard constantly at home.

65

Of course, her father's speech wasn't all that different from hers. He still spoke Jamaican, give or take a few patches of Yank here and there. But they didn't dare comment on the breadwinner. The Stewarts also spoke English when they felt like it.

Brenda started using English all the time to Lyn and Johnnie and only spoke patwa at the bakery. That felt like a kind of secret victory as far as she was concerned, because they still spoke Black American talk. Whenever she answered the phone, they would look at each other and their friends invariably wanted to know who that speaker was.

Brenda read everything in sight. Joan told her she could borrow any book from the shelves, as long as she wrote her name in the little black notebook on her desk. She should cross out her name when she returned a book. Many of them were stories set in Jamaica and the other Caribbean islands. Those were the stories she had not found in the school library, no matter how hard she looked. Others were American stories she had come to like. Between the lessons from Joan Stewart and the books she was reading, Brenda's English compositions soon became the ones the teacher selected for reading to class as examples of this and that. And everybody in the class wanted her to discuss the literature homework with them before the teachers started. Especially if poetry was a part of it.

Brenda really blossomed in High School. Lessons were easy. She had conquered the humanities, and as for the sciences, she had a distinct advantage there. Physics and chemistry learned in High School in Jamaica stood her in good stead when these subjects were introduced in Grade Ten. The teachers said she was very bright, as if this was the most shocking fact in the world.

The next winter was indeed milder. In any case, Brenda was so taken up with her school work and her after-school job that she hardly noticed that kind of discomfort. And spring seemed to come round again with amazing speed.

In the spring, the bakery netball team began to practise. Netball was not an American game, but the West Indians played it there just as they played cricket and dominoes. Brenda had been on the junior team at school in Jamaica.

She told Mrs Stewart she wanted to play and started training with the team every Saturday afternoon. Brenda played a strong centre. She was the youngest on the team, but it soon became clear that they couldn't do without her. One Saturday each month, they played against a team from Yonkers or some other nearby town with a heavy concentration of West Indians. Once they went to Hartford, Connecticut, to play the Jamaican team there. Imagine her surprise when she found a girl from her form in Jamaica, playing on their team! She too had migrated, but both her parents were there and she had a brother and sister. She and Brenda promised to keep in touch by telephone. Brenda enjoyed herself so much she couldn't fall asleep when she came home. She just kept going over the day in her mind.

The year Brenda finished high school, the Jamaican Association of New York sponsored a competition for the best essay written by someone under nineteen on "The Jamaica I remember". The prize was a trip to Jamaica. Brenda won the prize. It was a fourteen-day ticket and she could keep it to be used during the summer. She bought an extra copy of the school yearbook with a picture of herself receiving the prize from the president of the association. There was a write up about her, with everything about her scholastic and extra-curricular activities. She took a copy home for her mother.

Miss Chambers told her boss her daughter had won a prize trip home and asked to have her annual leave then.

Her mother had been so happy to see her that Brenda was embarrassed. She hadn't known her mother to be a boastful person. She hadn't gone out of her way to tell people when Brenda passed the coveted Common Entrance and entered High School, but she was bragging shamelessly now about the prize trip that had brought her one child home. Everybody who came to the house had to see the yearbook. And once or twice, when she pretended to be sleeping, she had caught her mother looking at her with strangely solemn eyes.

Chapter IX   MamaJoy

Joy Chambers knew that this return, this success, was what God had chosen for telling her the decision had been right. It hadn't been easy for her to send her only child to Ivan. She didn't even know the man. She hadn't known the boy. The young man who had taken a farmwork ticket to run away without a word when she got pregnant could hardly be the childhood sweetheart she thought she knew. That they had been friends so long had made the whole thing doubly hurtful. She had been duped by a smart man in boy's clothing. They had been together as long as she could remember. In the same Sunday school class and the same Young People's Association in the church. They used to call him Jack Sprat and call her His Wife because he was so thin, though she wasn't really fat.

She hadn't been a wild girl. Somebody said somewhere that the wild ones never get pregnant because they are always prepared. And it wasn't the first time. The first time had been very painful, and left her all bruised up and sore for a good long time. After that, it didn't hurt. Not to say it was a regular thing at all. They had decided that it wasn't wrong, but that big people just didn't understand or had chosen to forget. They would do it whenever they got the chance. She told herself that if it was something he had to do she would rather he did it with her. There were several takers anxious and ready if she said no. The chance always had to do with his parents' Members' Meeting.

Of course, they would take precautions. Nothing too fancy, just the rhythm method she had heard that the Roman Catholics used; and to make quite sure, he would stop before the danger point. 'Are you sure you can manage it?' she had asked, and he had said, 'Of course, it only takes a little self control.'

The day she did the last paper in the Third Year exam had been a Friday – Members' Meeting. The afternoon they had had a day party at school. It was a fund-raising event for the

school library. They had danced a lot. Close. He didn't have to ask. He only said, 'Thank God it's Friday.'

He didn't stop himself quick enough this time. It got away, he said. But she really didn't think anything would happen the one little time. She groaned out loud in her reverie.

'What happen, MamaJoy?' Brenda, immediately awake, asked her.

'Nothing, my dear, just sighing.'

'MamaJoy, go to your bed now. We have a long day to-morrow.'

'Mhm,' she said, and kept on sitting there.

When Ivan said he wanted the child in America, she was mad vex. Not her one child that she suck salt for. Ivan must be think fifty dollars every now and then can buy somebody. At first, she didn't say anything about it to Brenda. And she didn't send to answer him, either. She thought about it for several weeks, then decided that it would be selfish not to send her, since she would get free university education there and a much bigger choice of what to do with her life.

Her own mother didn't approve at all. Say Ivan didn't deserve the child. Say is only when she get big and bright him decide to want her. Tell her Brenda will forget her. Ask her if she know what might happen. She might get education and more. Like what happen to her. Joy had laughed a terrible laugh then, and said what happened to her happened right under her parents' nose and that nobody had raped her. In any case, she said, she had already told Brenda everything because they live in Kingston and is a fast city. She knew that the main thing was that her mother didn't want to lose the granddaughter. But it had worked. Look at Brenda. Of course, something could still happen, but, oh God, no. She sighed out loud again.

'MamaJoy, what happen? You getting nightmares. Go to your bed now man. Poor you. Brain working overtime. Go to sleep.'

Joy finally got up from the chair. Her eyes were wet. She didn't know whether it was joy or grief. Emotion anyway. She was mopping her eyes as she went towards the bedroom.

Granny Chambers thanked God over and over for the miracle, explaining to Him and to Brenda that she had

thought she would never see her grandchild again. When she heard of Mrs Stewart's part in the whole thing, she raised her eyes to the skies and quoted loudly, 'Cast they bread upon the waters and thou shalt find it after many days.'

With the help of the girl in Hartford, who seemed to be a great writer of letters and knew everybody's phone number, Brenda had managed to track down a few of the girls she had known in High School. She had never been good at correspondence, and after Christmas cards the first year, she had not written any of them. But they took her to Hellshire for fish and festival one Saturday, and she went with them on a hike to Cinchona, a place she had never heard about when she lived in Jamaica.

She was shocked at how happy these girls were. She wasn't sure what she had expected. They didn't seem worried about their education, either. They were in Sixth Form and would go to university or do something else. One of them already had a heavy schedule in modelling. Brenda was glad that she had been doing so well and had her little job with Mrs Stewart. Otherwise, she would definitely have felt deprived.

Chapter X   Changes

She should have known something unexpected would happen. She had been too happy in Jamaica. Her grandmother, the same one Mrs Stewart knew, used to say, 'Chicken merry hawk de near.' But she had felt no premonition.

It was still bright outside when the plane touched down at JFK. Brenda got out of the customs hall in record time and went down the stairs to get the airport bus. Her father was waiting at the exit door. She was surprised. He hadn't said anything about coming to meet her.

As usual, he had said very little to her about anything. Even the prize. He had congratulated her, of course, when she won it, but he had behaved at the bakery as if it was nothing special. She didn't know whether he didn't want to seem too proud in front of his co-workers, or whether he didn't think the achievement was all that much. She thought he was a strange man. He took her suitcase and started to walk towards the car park.

'I know you didn't expect me,' he said, 'but I wanted to talk to you before you go home.' Brenda said nothing. There was an uncomfortable pause and he continued: 'Johnnie and Lyn not there.'

'How come? Why?'

'Johnnie and me part.'

'What?'

'We part. We are not together anymore.'

'What happen?'

'I was talking to somebody else and she find out. Saturday I went out, and when I come back, all the furniture gone and the things leave on the floor.'

'So she didn't warn you or anything?'

'No, and she don't even leave a note to say where she gone.' He didn't bother to tell Brenda about the joint account she had cleaned out, or his luck in having some money in a private account she didn't know anything about.

Brenda sat next to him in the front of the car, but found

herself unable to say anything for a long time. She felt she should say she was sorry, but in the years they had lived under the same roof, the relationship between herself and those two had not improved. It had deteriorated, if that was possible. And she and her father had never discussed it.

'So what you have to say?' her father asked.

'Nothing. You going to move from the apartment?'

'No.'

'So what is in there now?'

'I bought a few second hand things so we can stay in it. Your things are in your room, but it chaka-chaka.'

A regular job at the bakery was awaiting her return. That was the plan. She had done a computer course as part of her high school programme. Mrs Stewart's decision to computerize the office operations, then, was partly because she was planning to hire her. She would get two hundred dollars a week and her lunch. While she was in Jamaica, she decided to save to buy her mother a new fridge. The current one was at least as old as she, and it showed. There were also a few small things she intended to send for her and for her grandmother the next time Mrs Stewart was going down.

Things moved very quickly after that. It seemed to Brenda that her father was serious about the new lady or she about him. She wanted him to come to England, and he couldn't find any good reason not to. The precious college education she had been brought to America to get didn't seem important anymore. In fact, he had gone and talked to his boss. He knew that her brother had the same kind of bakery business in England, in Birmingham. She talked to her brother, and Ivan started planning to go to Birmingham. The lady was a nurse in London, but she said she would get a transfer as soon as he came over.

They didn't stay long in the apartment. Mrs Stewart suggested that Brenda live with them the whole summer, and as long after as was necessary. One of the boys had left home. His room was empty. She would make her pay one tenth of her salary for room and board. Ivan gave up the apartment and got a room in a residential hotel for the few weeks, then left for Birmingham.

Brenda had to prepare to make the transition to the British education system. The new lady friend was a great help and sent a lot of material which Brenda and Mrs Stewart spent hours poring over.

She would have to enrol in a further education college. You couldn't just leave High School in New York and go to university in England. She would have to have A Level subjects. They wrote for a correspondence course so Brenda could start to prepare. She would sit the exams as soon as she went over there.

Brenda felt that she had no control over her life. She had come to understand America, at least New York. She had her niche now, thanks to Mrs Stewart. The Netball Club had opened up a social life for her. And even at school, she had made a few friends. They had applied to the same colleges for admission. She didn't really want to leave, but she knew that she would have to follow her father. She didn't want to leave the Stewarts, although Mrs Stewart tried to tell her that England wasn't bad. She herself had been educated there, and nothing was wrong with it except for the fog and rain. In fact, if she wanted to go back to Jamaica, it was probably a better place to get her education than America.

Staying with the Stewarts made all the difference in the world at a time when she felt the need for support.

Between work, study and netball, the year went quickly. She stayed on for the summer, working and saving all that she made. At the end of August, she left the Stewarts. Mrs Stewart was as sorry to lose her as she was sorry to have to go. Brenda had become her right-hand man in the office, efficient and entirely trustworthy and with a loyalty nothing could shake.

Amidst many parting tears, she left to join her father and his new lady in Birmingham. She was tense at the thought of another adjustment to a different home and a different school.

Chapter XI   No Sun

'Inglan iz a bitch,' Brenda found herself murmuring, over and over as if Kwesi Johnson had written the words specially for her. The summer was over. Not officially, as geography books go. But certainly in Birmingham the September she got there. It never seemed to stop raining. She remembered her first year in New York and how cold she had felt by November. She was numb with premonition. What would the Birmingham November be like?

She soon knew. True to everything the poets had written, the bleak month moved in, without sun, without moon, without dawn, without dusk, without proper time of day, especially without sun. No wonder people spoke about and wrote about the weather so much. It was THE thing to remark upon.

She found England uncomfortable. Inside and outside. It never got as cold outside as it did in America, but it felt colder. Perhaps that was because it rained so much and looked bleak. Inside, there was no central heating. At least, where they lived. A coin-operated heater warmed the area a few feet around it. And when she went to sleep, she had to be careful not to turn too much, for there was always a cold part of the bed waiting to trap her.

The bathroom was another trial. She found that you couldn't just turn on two taps and get warm water from hot mixed with cold. You had to do the mixing yourself. This made a big difference. Either you bathed in the tub or mixed your water in a pail. The pail reminded her of Jamaica. At least, of Birthright where her grandmother lived and everybody took a pail to the standpipe for water. There was no shower and she didn't feel comfortable using the tub. Everybody in the house had to use it. She never felt it was really clean. Somehow, this was different from the wooden tub she used to bathe in at her grandmother's house. She never felt that was dirty. Perhaps because of the loving care with which her grandmother would set it outside so the water could get warm for her bath. Her prejudice was illogical. She knew it. Nevertheless, she religiously stood in the tub, soaped her body thoroughly, then poured the mixed water from the pail all over her.

They didn't have a washing machine. She had to take the clothes to the launderette in all kinds of weather. Quite soon, she decided that the English people who went to America had migrated because they wanted a little comfort. She wondered how her father made the transition so easily. He seemed so comfortable in the half-cold place with Nurse who, true to her word, had left her London job and moved to work in Birmingham and live with him as she had promised.

Brenda had to admit that this woman was more pleasing to her than Johnnie. In fact, there was no comparison. Her voice was softer. She had hated the high-pitched shrillness of Johnnie's voice. And she had no Lyn. Home was OK in terms of atmosphere.

Brenda took care of the washing. And didn't mind. She never had to cook. Nurse took pride in cooking for her father, cooking all the Jamaican food they had missed in Johnnie's house. And he brought home patties and gizadas from time to time, and the coco-bread that Nurse loved.

* * *

At school, at the College of Further Education, called the FE College, she wasn't comfortable. Apart from being new, she had two strokes against her. She was black and she spoke English with an American accent. She felt that the teachers didn't like her, that they were prejudiced in spite of their smiling. And the students, the black ones who were mostly Jamaicans, didn't want to talk to her much. Perhaps her shyness and insecurity came over to them as stand-offishness. If they had let her into their little groups, they would have found out that nothing was wrong with her. She didn't even know that she spoke English with an American accent. And her patwa was as good as theirs. One day, as she was answering a question in class, she actually heard one of them whisper, 'A wa she a play,' as if they thought she had cultivated her accent. That set her back even further. She went right back into her shell.

She would have to start all over again with the social side of life. Try to make new friends. And there was no church

75

community this time. And, of course, no Mrs Stewart. A part of her decided that she was there to pass A Levels and she wasn't about to bother with anything else. But it wasn't so easy. She was lonely for company her own age. She felt the prejudice of some of the teachers, and because she was older and more sophisticated, she could recognize it. She didn't have the sympathy of the group when the teachers were picking on her. Not that they didn't pick on other black students, but *they* had the psychological support of their friends. She felt very isolated, and simply buried herself in her books.

Even at home, she didn't talk much. Her father and Nurse spent all the time they had talking to each other. Sometimes, he worked late, and sometimes, she worked at night, but whenever they were at home together, he was with her. Even when she was in the kitchen cooking, he was hovering over her. He was a far more relaxed man than he had been in America.

Brenda missed the Stewarts. She didn't know she would miss them so much, especially Mrs Stewart, who could so easily sense her moods and her needs. Nurse probably felt that she was a big girl or was fooled by her external composure. She found an afternoon babysitting job quite near to where they lived, so she didn't have to ask her father for pocket money. Her first purchase was an electric blanket.

She had no choice but to study hard. She got her three A Levels and a sizeable grant to go to university. She had looked at the bulletin boards and applied for all the available grants and scholarships, just as Mrs Stewart had told her to.

*   *   *

During her last term at the FE College, Brenda had met Laura. A lecturer had been ill and this bright young Jamaican postgraduate student turned up to take his lectures. Social history. After the last of the classes, Laura had suggested they have a cup of tea in the cafeteria and they chatted a little. She was staying with her uncle and aunt who had lived in Birmingham for twenty years. Brenda and her father had only recently arrived. The conversation didn't get much

deeper than that, though Laura did give her some pointers about selecting courses once she got into a university.

A year or so later, just before Christmas, Brenda met Laura again at an African Studies get-together at the Africa Centre. Most black students turned up at these parties. African meant all diaspora people. The music was good. The West Indians danced to Nigerian and Ghanaian music as if they were born hearing it. The food was near enough to West Indian food to be good, and far enough from it to be exotic. Brenda was having a good time, but she didn't have one positive word to say about her experience in England so far. Laura was more than a little surprised that somebody who was coming from America where, as far as she had heard, prejudice was rampant, should find England so difficult.

'So, you would say it is worse here than in New York?'

'Maybe it's not fair to compare them. Maybe when I was in the States I was younger. I don't know. Besides, I was so unhappy at home in New York that a lot of my energy went into dealing with that. Let me think about it and try to give you a sensible answer. I don't know why, but I find myself not able to trust these people. If they smile with me, I don't think they mean it.'

'And you think the Americans meant it more?'

'Well, I had learnt to read their faces, I believe. The white teachers had a way of smiling at you in school where they bared their teeth and nothing happened in their eyes. I would just say in my mind, 'All kin teet a no laugh,' and ignore them, but here they persist in trying to be so charming. Maybe I was prejudiced against them from before I came. I don't know. My grandmother used to say the Englishman will shake your hand and go and wash his afterwards while the American won't shake it at all. Did you ever hear that?'

'No,' Laura laughed. 'But I understand the point.'

'Of course, my dear grandmother has been to neither England nor America.'

'I figure. But what about the lecturers? How is the work?'

'That part is OK, you know. I have my own agenda which they can't mess with. It's just that I get tired of having to look out for where they are coming from every time. Don't get me wrong, you know. Some of them are OK.'

'Yes,' said Laura, 'as in, "some of my best friends are black"'

'You said it!'

'So you don't have any Jamaican friends?'

'My dear, when I came here and went to the FE College where you found me, as soon as I opened my mouth the Jamaicans proceeded to laugh at me. It took me a little time to find out that they thought I was putting on how I talk. I didn't even realize I had an American accent, and they never talked to me enough to hear that I sound just like them when I talk patwa, so I just kept myself to myself and that's how it has remained. I talk to a few people my age in the building where I live, but they are mostly from the other islands and all of them are working, not studying, so their hours are sort of different from mine.'

'You must be very lonely, then.'

'I would say that.'

'You want to come for Saturday soup at my house?'

'You mean tomorrow Saturday?'

'Yes. Why, you busy?'

'No. Only the library. What time you were thinking about?'

'About three or four.'

'OK. I should finish at the library around that time myself. Can we meet in the first floor lobby at 3.30? It's only about fifteen minutes by bus at that time.'

'You have a telephone?'

'Mhmm.'

'Just in case. If I can't make it, I will call you Saturday morning.'

'Here is the number.'

Brenda had come by that afternoon and enjoyed herself. Edith had made a beef soup second only to what Brenda's grandmother was capable of. It was just right for the chilly evening. David had been in his element. All the political problems of the world had been solved in the living room after soup.

The Saturday soup became a ritual till a Saturday afternoon seminar got on Laura's agenda. They lost each other. Laura's conscience had bothered her a bit. But it was soon after that that she had fallen into a very demanding love, and had to juggle that with a very demanding work schedule. She was

trying not to lose her head and to milk the time she had dry. She was reading every journal she could find and going to every public lecture in her field. She had been sent abroad because none of it was available at home.

It was near the end of Brenda's second year, her last, that Laura became aware that Brenda had moved to the fringes of a radical group. She seemed to have found a niche. Laura told herself that was a good thing and to let her conscience rest. Any crowd was better than no crowd, particularly in a university setting. They weren't her type, but she herself thought there was no special virtue in being like her and her crowd. The times she glimpsed Brenda she was in full African regalia. She had allowed her hair to go dread and was in the company of young men who constantly looked very intense and gesticulated wildly. She looked involved, though. In whatever it was. Nothing like the luke-warm, unimpressed young woman she had talked to a year earlier. And, from time to time, she would recognize her name in a list of scribblers reading their work at poetry meetings.

So much had happened in her own life between that time and the airport meeting, Laura had no idea what Brenda might have got up to.

PART III

Chapter XII Laura's Jamaica

There were two good dresses in the closet. The little black, which everybody knew, and the green with the peplum. A slightly more sporty look. Laura chose the latter. People always said she looked light-hearted in it. The black was just a little too formal.

Her friend Carol was dead on time. Even so, they had to park two blocks away from the hotel. Both car parks were full. As soon as they entered the hotel, they knew why. The bulletin board said that lawyers were having cocktails in one of the suites.

The door was open as they passed. One could tell by the clothes that these were people who earned money. Somebody said, 'Hi.' Laura was surprised she recognized one of them.

At the door to the Sam Sharpe suite, somebody took their tickets and pinned corsages on them. Almost immediately, a waiter came by with a tray of drinks. Both of them started with fruit punch. They would move slowly up to strong. The second was white wine. They were already enjoying the evening. Laura said she was surprised. Carol felt vindicated. She had dragged her long-time friend to an old students' do and had promised her a good time. Second drink at the door, and already there were faces they both recognized, although Laura hadn't seen some of them in the dozen or so years since she left school. Progress towards the table with their number on it was slow, as every next person stopped them. Carol knew someone in every group they passed. The guests of honour were in the foyer, so one felt the urge to greet them. Eventually, they were seated, but it was obvious the proceedings were a long way from beginning.

Laura swung her chair around to try to take in who and who were sitting at the table next to her, and her eyes immediately made four with Brenda, just settling in beside a woman Laura recognized immediately from the

famous Amazones sixth form, from which both she and Carol had graduated. Brenda was looking really well. And calm. No sign of the wretched hypercritical girl who came off the plane that afternoon. Of course, she hadn't spoken to her yet. Her hair was pulled back then brought forward in a pile, so that what had appeared to be untidy rat-tails then were now an elegant coiffeur. She was wearing one of those understated black dresses, a bit like the one Laura had decided against. Obviously, she was not playing the young hothead nor the angry returnee tonight.

Laura went over. They didn't see her approach.

'Hi!' The two girls swivelled their chairs around and both of them called her name in one of those stage shouts that express surprise.

'You know each other?' asked Brenda.

'Do we?' asked Laura.

'Brenda, where do you know this woman from?'

'You really want to know? We are blood. Her mother is my father's cousin. And besides, we are friends.'

'So tell me, Miss Jackson, what have you been up to? Are you still Jackson?'

'Yes to the second of those, and to the first, nothing much.' They traded job information.

'And you, Miss Brenda. Why did I think you were going to call me?' Laura felt a little like a fraud when she said that. She hadn't really been looking forward to the call.

'It's not late. Shall we make a definite date?'

'Mhm. What about lunch at Devon House next week Saturday, at noon?'

'Fine by me.'

'It's a deal.'

'In case you wanted to invite me, I can't make it' Jessica Jackson said.

'My apologies, Ms Jackson,' said Laura, acknowledging her poor manners. 'Come along no'!'

'No. Seriously. I'll be out of town.'

Laura returned to the table and sat next to the chair Carol was to desert over and over again to go and talk with this one or that one. The dinner was formal only in the sense that you sat at a table. Carol had taught at the school for a

few years, so she knew that many people more than Laura did and kept going to greet them.

The occasion was a very moving one. Tributes were read to the ten people being honoured, mostly teachers. A few were individuals who were performing other kinds of useful service out there in the world. And there was a special tribute to the headmaster, old and shaky now, looking older than Laura remembered his father to look in the old days when she was a student.

The meal was not spectacular, but the company was. One recognized so many faces from all parts of the community – people who were doing their jobs well and people who were giving voluntary service. Laura felt proud that she had something in common with this bunch.

There was a brief break between the meal and the entertainment. It was a real galaxy of entertainers, representing different eras of popular music. All of them had attended the school at some time over the last twenty years. Laura felt her head swell. Some of these were children to her. Others were much older. They were all very very talented. It came to an end too soon with the youngest of the entertainers, a successful jazz singer about twenty-two years old. She dedicated a song to Carol, who had taught her and who had given her the freedom to recognize, she said, her special talent, although it was not academic.

Everybody was on a high. Laura and Carol decided that they couldn't go home like that. They went over to ask Brenda and Jessica if they wanted to finish the night at a jazz club. Laura suggested Daddyrock, and nobody had any objection.

The music was good. But too loud for people to talk through. The room was small and full of smoke. For some reason, there was no restriction on that. The saxophonist was superb, the other players adequate. They left the club at about two in the morning, Laura reminding Brenda about their date.

'I'll be there,' said Brenda. 'This St Anne's mafia has me feeling quite jealous, though. What happen to those of us who didn't go to school there?'

'You name Bat,' said Laura, and hurried off.

Chapter XIII   Claiming the rock

On Saturday, slightly after noon, Brenda stepped out of the taxi, paid the driver and immediately found her hair entangled in a bougainvillea bush she was too slow to avoid. Untangling herself, she kept thinking that she was getting later and later, and that she was the one who should be prompt. Wasn't she the one who lived in England?

Free at last, she ran along the concrete, ignoring the shops on either side and even the wares under the tree as the end-of-month sale progressed. People were sitting in twos and threes on stone benches in shady alcoves which looked like arbours for some fruit she didn't know. Laura was waving from the balcony. She was sipping a drink, and obviously trying to look relaxed as if her patience was not being tested.

'Sorry to be late,' Brenda said, and resisted the urge to advance a lame excuse.

'It's all right. I usually start with coconut water anyway. They say it washes your kidneys.'

'I'll have a kidney wash, too.'

The waiter brought the menus and went back for Brenda's coconut water.

'And another for me,' Laura shouted, and in a lower voice she continued, 'my kidneys are very dirty.'

Brenda took the menu. 'You advise me, Laura, what does the ackee quiche taste like? I always think white people have the knack of making over everything in their image – Europeanizing it. Ackee is to go with saltfish and ripe pear.'

'I used to think that too, you know, but I myself play so many tricks with the recipes in their books, I don't dare forbid them to experiment with my material. In any case, they wouldn't listen. Whoever started it, the person carrying it on in this place is a full-blooded Jamaican woman. And an excellent cook.'

'OK, I'll try that, but I will have potato pudding for dessert. I have no fear about that.'

'Me too. About the potato pudding. And they make the best in Jamaica, except perhaps for everybody's grandmother. I will have mushroom quiche. I don't apologize for the tastes I picked up abroad. I l-o-v-e mushrooms. Afterwards, we will sit in the alcove and lick a cone, if you don't mind. This is one place I don't watch my weight.'

'As if you have to.'

'My dear, a bulge shows more on a pin than on an elephant. Anyway, you shouldn't talk. So tell me what exactly you are up to. What are you doing here? I couldn't ask you anything the day in the airport, you were too uptight.'

'This seems like so long ago now. I don't mean I'm not still uptight, but . . .'

'Mhmm, a little less so. I know. Far less so. I can feel that. You're doing research?'

'In a manner of speaking. I work for this small journal. Calls itself Yard. It's really West Indians trying to find a place to educate themselves and the community around them about the islands. They want to do something on Heritage and they want me to write a feature on Jamaica. So I will be here till the end of October.'

'Tell me something. And excuse my frankness, but why they sent you when you feel so negative about this place? I mean, after I left the taxi that day, I really started to look around me.'

'Truth is, they didn't have much choice. They needed somebody with the time and the interest. It had to be somebody who would spend from August to October in Jamaica and not mind. And they like the way I write. It was a Godsend for me. I hadn't seen my mother in a very long time and she needed my help particularly at this time. She is getting ready to make some changes in her life.

'I have never, as an adult, been around for Heritage Week. I had been here for a few weeks in July one time when I was living in New York and won a prize ticket. And I remember Festival and Independence from my schooldays here.

'The chance to come home has come to me very rarely,' she added, shaking her head; and with a wry smile, she said, 'I'm not like you, you know. Big scholarship and all.'

'So what, you were paying for yourself at Birmingham?

I thought you were on scholarship,' said Laura, knowing perfectly well that she was.

'Yes .... Just kidding,' Brenda said, blowing a ring of smoke in the air and trying to avoid its polluting Laura's air directly. She decided she would stop at the one cigarette. Laura was clearly uncomfortable.

'I am glad they sent me,' Brenda resumed. 'First thing is the time I am spending with my mother. We needed to spend time together and could never afford the fare. Besides, she is building a flat onto the townhouse. Frankly, I don't know how she would have managed without me to sit on the workmen round the clock. Talk about work attitudes. Tell me something, Laura, what are production levels like in this country?'

'Well below the English standard, I suppose,' Laura said.

'I am glad you have the grace to blush. Seriously though, if these workmen are any indication we, yes, I suppose we, have problems. Anyway, let's not talk about that. But all of that is part of what I am dealing with. For among other things, I am trying to come to terms with this rock and to sort of claim it again.

'I know you think I am hypercritical. Almost as if I hate it. I have been thinking about that a lot too. Attending festival activities, watching hundreds of children performing in a way it must have taken teachers with the patience of Job to get them to perform. And I know how much teachers earn. There is a lot of commitment here still.

Then the Alumni affair and watching how passionately you all feel about St Anne's, no matter what else you have experienced, was very sobering. I believe half of my rejection of Jamaica . . .'

'Rejection?'

'Yes, rejection . . . is a feeling deep down that it rejected *me*, and gave me what? England and America. And then the few times I have come, this place seems so disorganized compared with them that, again, I resent that. Almost as if I am saying, "Look how inept you are, and you spat me out. Can't even clean up your act." Then of course I resent America and England, especially England where I was most conscious. Look, it is too difficult, I can't explain it. I am just trying to work it out myself.'

'Go on. But tell me first: didn't you feel glad to go to America? When I was in school, everybody wanted to go.'

'Hell, yes. But did you talk to any of them AFTER they got there?'

'No.'

'You don't understand. When you reached England, you had already finished a first degree and you were living with your relatives. I went to America to a father I didn't know and a stepmother who hated me. By the time I got comfortable there with the help of a good fairy, I had to go to England. When I went to that FE College where you saw me, I was being snubbed for my American accent. I am sure YOU found friends from among the same types that were rejecting me. I don't know what they have against Blacks from America, anyway.'

'Brenda, I'm sorry,' said Laura, leaning over and taking both Brenda's hands in her own. 'I really hadn't realized it was so bad. I must let you meet Georgia. She studied in America, and tells terrible tales about that division over there and how we have fed right into it. Can you see what a force black people could be if we united? On both sides of the Atlantic? That's why they try so hard to divide us. It's a strategy as old as time.'

'I understand the politics of it, but at the time all I knew was that I was miserable. Remember, I didn't go to High School here, you know – not after Third Form. It was a terrible scene there. It took every day of my time there to get my head together, and just as I did that, my father was ready to move to England.'

'Try to tell me what was so bad about America.'

'For one thing, I didn't expect the loneliness. Somehow, I hadn't bargained on a stepmother and stepsister, especially ones who hated me. And my father wasn't there for me.'

'How you mean?'

'It's not really his fault. I don't think he had any idea what a fourteen-year-old in a strange country required. And he obviously had his own problems, living with a woman from another culture and a totally undisciplined stepchild. Perhaps he couldn't talk to me because he hadn't been talking to her, and he didn't want to treat one different from the other. He

89

just didn't talk to me more than was absolutely necessary. Then the school thing. I wasn't a dunce. I had been bright at school up till then. But they made the things you didn't know seem so large . . . you became not just minority but downright inferior. If you couldn't pass the little tests which, now I look back on them, were severely culture-bound, you had a problem. You know what eventually saved me? An evening job with my father's employer. I'm sure she didn't need me, but she saw my dilemma and wanted to help. She is from Porus and knows my grandmother. She got her daughter to help me with my lessons when I was supposed to be working. God bless her. I graduated from High School with straight As after a very inauspicious Junior High career. I don't know what would have happened if she hadn't intervened. It is she who sent for the correspondence course so I could start preparing for my A Levels before I reached England.

'I don't even like to remember the FE College. Things started looking better at the university. I was mixing with Africans and with West Indians from different islands. I had sort of given up on Jamaicans by then. The politics was new to me. I hadn't been at all political before. Everything was an issue. I was excited. Something terrible was always happening in one part of Africa or the other. And whenever there was nothing special, there was always South Africa. I felt cosy. I was a part of something. You must have thought me weird, then, with my pseudo Africanness, clothes and all.'

'Not really. Different, but not weird.'

'That's kind.'

'In fact, I have always wondered what made black people living in England so conscious about so many causes. Certainly a lot of those I met at university. Perhaps it's just me, but my own response has always been lukewarm compared with theirs. I never knew what was happening in which part of Africa, except perhaps South Africa. Perhaps I should be ashamed.'

'Perhaps not. Maybe there are other important things you are interested in that they are not.'

'I very much doubt it, but continue YOUR story.'

'After university, it was the job market. That was something

90

else. Pray that you never have to face those people across a table. They have one place for you in their minds, the ground floor. You know, where the mops and brooms are kept? I just didn't have the stamina to deal with it. They made my Upper Second feel like sawdust in my hands. I hurried back to Academia and begged the head of English to take me in. I got a grant, wrote up a proposal and remained in the shelter for two more years. They even made me a sub-warden, so I had my own flat. Then I got tired of the university. They couldn't persuade me to stay for a PhD.

'OK, that's not really the whole story. I had to get out of that environment. There's an emotional part which I don't want to talk about.'

'Fair enough.'

'In any case, I went out there again. This time I was more choosy. I signed up to be a trainee editor with a big publishing house. Didn't pay anything much, just enough to keep me going. I made some contacts there and started freelancing. The rest is history.'

'So how has that gone?'

'So so. This is the best break I have had. And I intend to make it worth their while. They pay me well. I gave up my little apartment and stored my things in my father's place. That makes things even better financially. I must say, he has been pretty decent. They have a house now. He and Nurse, who is his wife now. I have a room in the house and he doesn't mind how I use it. The fact that Nurse doesn't have any children helps, I believe.'

'Let's go for the cone.'

'Good. I want rum and raisin.'

'Next time you must try a fruit flavour. Soursop or coconut.'

'Why not now? Which you recommend?'

'They will give you a taste of each if you want and you can make up your mind. Or you can have a double. I do that when I can't decide.'

Sitting in the alcove afterwards on one of the stone benches she had passed on her way in, Brenda had to admit this was the longest, finest lunch she had had in a long time.

'I could live with this pace,' she said.

'That's the reason I am here,' said Laura, 'beside the weather, of course, and the music, and . . .'

'Point taken.'

'Before I forget, Brenda, my family is having a get-together the Sunday of Heritage Week. I will leave straight from there to Mento Yard, of which I hope you have heard?'

'Yes, man, I have to go to that anyway.'

'How were you getting there?'

'I don't know. I was going to go to the festival office to find out what they advise.'

'You want to come with me? You would have to sleep over, though. Remember my aunt and uncle from Birmingham?'

'Of course. How could I forget that soup and that sense of humour? Isn't your uncle the one whose friend had two shirts, one numbered ten and one seventeen?'

'Same one. They live here now.'

'Since when?'

'About a year.'

'And how are they adjusting? Didn't they live there a very long time?'

'Thirty years. You'll be able to judge. Consider yourself invited for the long weekend.'

'That's super. What have I done to deserve this luck?'

'Just sleep tonight on the same side you slept on last night.'

It had begun to rain slightly. The drops started to get heavy.

'Finish your cone in the car,' Laura said. 'Hope Road is hopeless when it rains.'

'All right. Can I tell you how much I appreciate this lunch? I mean lunch and therapy.'

'No. Put it in writing,' Laura said, with mock seriousness.

Chapter XIV   Edaville

'You haven't seen St Mary's hills,' Laura said.

'Nooo,' said Brenda through a huge yawn, stretching her limbs taut as far as space in the car would allow.

'You slept through the whole forty miles. We're almost at Woods. Look, there's the village down there. Anybody who can sleep over the Junction road with all those corners must be really tired.'

'I AM tired. I've been going non-stop since you saw me last. Since Independence, in fact. Nobody would believe there is so much to do in Kingston. This week in particular. I have been to more Heritage Week things than you could possibly have heard about. And the heat exhausts me.'

The car crossed over to the right and pulled up sharply near the bank. There was barely space for a very thin person to get out on the driver side. But that was the only way to park if the car wasn't to be hit by the first bus taking the corner. Trunk and crown of healthy coconut trees were immediately visible with leaves glistening in the morning sun.

'What happen, lethal yellowing didn't reach here? I thought they said it was the whole of St Mary.'

'Sheer luck, my dear,' Laura said, as she squeezed her way out of the car. They walked into the yard through the open gate. Zeeland, the yard man, was standing there with a cutlass, obviously ready to cut water coconuts sitting in bunches at his feet. He smiled broadly as they approached.

'Maas Zee, how you do?'

'So so, Miss Laura, and you?'

'Not too bad. Meet a friend of mine. She is here from England.'

'Please to meet you, Miss . . .?

'Brenda.'

'Pleased to meet you, Miss Brenda.'

'Pleased to meet you too, Maas Zee.'

'You want coconut water, Brenda?'

'Of course.'

'Cut two for us there, Maas Zee. Brenda, how you like the inside, hard or soft?'

'Medium.'

'Medium for me, too.'

'Two medium, Maas Zee.'

Brenda started to laugh.

'What you laughing about?' Laura wanted to know.

'Just the sight of the coconut tree and the natives underneath cutting and drinking. I mean, I know these nuts didn't come from these trees, but the whole thing is out of a tourist brochure. I mean, nobody expects it to be quite like this.'

Edith had seen them entering the yard and had started walking towards them over the uneven surface. By the time they had guzzled down the water and scooped the coconut meat out with Maas Zeek's man-made spoons, she had caught up with them.

'Aunt Edith, you remember Brenda, don't you?'

'Of course,' said Edith, showing her small even teeth as she smiled and hugged them both.

'Nice to see you again, Miss Edith,' said Brenda. 'I've never forgotten your Saturday soup.'

'Thank you, Brenda. Come on up. David is anxious to see you.'

David came out immediately, speaking as he came.

'Miss Brenda, welcome to our little home. Laura, how you do?'

'I wouldn't call this little, you know. Thanks for the welcome, though. Birmingham feels like hundreds of years away, doesn't it?'

'Tell you the truth, sometimes we don't remember it for days on end, no true, Edith?'

'You'd be surprised, you know, Brenda, how easy it is to forget.'

'I can understand,' Brenda said. 'I have been here two months and I feel as if I have been here forever, far less you who have walked right back into your home.'

Laura turned into the guest room and Brenda followed her.

'Please make yourself at home, Brenda,' Edith said.

'Thank you. I feel at home already.'

'Want any help, Aunt Edith?'

'No, my dear. Mabel and the girls have everything under control.'

'Mabel, how you do?' Laura shouted.

'Not bad, Miss Laura,' came back from the kitchen.

People began to arrive. First a trickle, then whole families, in some cases. Soon children were rushing up and down the hilly yard, going after different things to eat. Fruit was piled in small heaps – mango, orange, naseberry. There were bunches of ripe banana hanging from trees of all sorts. The children seemed to get a kick out of pulling them directly from the stem. There was cane with a young man to peel it, the way Zeeland was there for the coconuts. A tangerine tree in the front yard was laden with low hanging fruit, ripe and almost ripe. Close to it was a soursop tree with coconut drops on strings dangling from its branches. Drops were at mouth length for people only four feet tall. David's mango tree with cho chos hanging from it didn't look strange in this environment.

Woods Village is in limestone country. Here and there, rocks descend to openings which are mouths of small caves. Sticks with red flags on them had been stuck in the ground at each cave mouth, and banners reading, "DANGER – SINK HOLE" hung from branches of trees above each opening. Laura told Brenda that when she used to visit as a child, there were no flags there, but she had been so totally indoctrinated in the lore that the sink hole eventually led to the sea twelve miles away, there was no danger of her walking near to any of the areas where the rock sloped.

A truck arrived and delivered blocks of ice. Maas Zee had relinquished his post by the coconuts and was setting up a stall. A much younger man was standing in for him. Soon he came up to the house and collected bottle after bottle of what turned out to be ginger beer, passionfruit drink and syrup in red and orange. Children of varying heights were following him, pied piper from somewhere, all the way down the hill. Soon they would form an almost complete circle around him as he pushed the little metal machine over the ice resting on sawdust in a crocus bag. This was obviously new to them. They waited with uncharacteristic patience as one at a time

they received a snowball eased with his huge thumb out of the machine and covered with bright red or orange syrup. They they scampered off with syrup running along their hands all the way down to their elbows.

When Laura and Brenda reached the kitchen, Mabel was piling fried chicken onto two large trays. Laura lifted the cloth covering an anonymous tray on the kitchen counter. It had on it fried fish – sprat. Even Laura, who lived in Jamaica, had not tasted sprat in many many years.

'Sprat!' Brenda called out, and went into a reverie about her grandmother. Laura took a side plate from the shelf and put on it two small fish covered with onion and red pepper and dripping vinegar. She broke a piece off the hard "not-a-spring" bread and broke it in two so they could have a taste of bread and fish. She found a bread knife and sliced off the jagged edges her fingers had left, pushing the small pieces into her mouth in a kind of frenzy. Brenda's eyes were filled with water as she stuffed fish and bread into her mouth and mumbled, 'Good, good.'

David appeared from nowhere and remarked 'Anything that make you cry so can't be good to eat.'

'I'll let that pass, Maas D,' said Brenda.

Edith had gone to the gate, chiefly to welcome guests. There was really nothing for Laura to help to do. Girls from the group Edith taught each week were obviously thrilled to be doing an entertainment job.

On the other side of the yard, there was a large outdoor fire burning. Bulwark (of the pentecostal spirit) was supervising the boiling of an oil tin full of mannish water and another of boiled corn. Pots of curried goat, rice and boiled bananas sat nearby, each on its own three stones.

The yard was getting full. It seemed that every car in Jamaica was parked on the road. A small district easily looks overcrowded. Laura had done an excellent job of digging relatives and friends from out of the woodwork. She and David and Edith were occupied full time, greeting and hugging them. Laura tried to introduce Brenda to as many people as she could. People were falling on each other's necks as friends or relatives met after many years.

Soon, cliques started to form. Over-sixties who hadn't had

a chance to call on David and Edith since their return, people in their twenties and thirties, Laura's friends and relatives, children and grandchildren of these two groups. A little one four weeks old was sucking happily away at the mother, while his brother aged two was asleep on a couch.

It was an unusual production. Ancient items of Jamaican cuisine, some hardly remembered, were represented – dukunoo, gizada, puddings of every sort. Brenda recognized smells and flavours from her childhood, and her holidays in Birthright came flooding back.

The occasional loud slap on a table announced that domino games were in progress. There were two tables going. Charley was proclaiming loudly that anybody who wished could come and beat him. Younger men solemnly clutched a handful of these "cards" and looked at their hands, wrinkling their foreheads in deep concentration.

There were people lounging around in comfortable chairs or resting on fat pillows, from which they raised themselves by the elbow to make a contribution. Politics was being discussed hotly.

Brenda decided to stay away from this. She didn't know enough about the group to be sure she could comment without being taken too seriously. She had heard that politics could be a life-and-death matter, even in discussions. She had lost Laura somewhere between the fruits and the curried goat. No wonder. There were people there who had not seen her, some for five, some for ten years or more. Everybody wanted her attention.

She was thinking it would be nice to go for a walk up the road, take a mini tour of the district. She had seen at least two groups leaving on foot, but figured they were going to visit specific homes, so she had decided not to ask to tag along.

An older couple was coming towards her and she decided not to resist. They wanted to know if she was related to the family, and when she said she was not they were visibly relieved. They said they had been feeling that they were the only non-relatives around. They had been invited by one of the cousins. Their accent was easily recognizable by Brenda. Jamaican with a slight English overlay. She told them she

lived in London and they perked up immediately, identifying with her as fellow Jamaicans from England. They had lived in Bristol for many years and had recently returned to settle in Jamaica.

With no encouragement at all, the man and woman jostled with each other to tell her how difficult their settling-in had been. They had not returned to the place they had left from and easily confessed that they hadn't wanted to be near relatives, most of whom had not done well. They had bought into a housing scheme in St Catherine and complained about low water pressure and sometimes no water at all; about power outages and outrageously high bills; about transportation, because they still had not been able to clear the pick-up they had shipped. There was impossible paper work, much of which they did not understand. Then they said things were expensive; even the townhouse they bought had cost them a couple thousand dollars more than they had agreed on. And when they complained, everybody said escalation was something you automatically expected. So none of the others in the scheme wanted to join them in taking the developers to court.

She wasn't required to say anything. She only had to groan the obligatory "Mhmmm" to admit that she identified with their problems. Clearly, they were sent to shock her into reality, in case anyone made her believe David and Edith's was the typical experience. As if she didn't know better.

The cousin came to claim them. He wanted them to see the inside of the house. In any case, they were tired from the uphill and downhill movement for one kind of food or another. 'Gopaul luck a no Sepaul luck,' Brenda said, shaking her head as the couple left and trying to remember where she had first heard that. She was alone again and started to look around.

Chapter XV   Anthony

Sitting alone eating a large green guava was a young man to whom Laura had introduced Brenda earlier. He was a cousin living in the US, visiting for some reason, and lucky enough to be there for the celebration. Brenda went for a second mannish water, then walked up to him.

'Hi.'

'Hi.'

'What do you play?'

'Not dominoes.'

'Cards?'

'Limited to "Thanks" and "Strip me", the versions that were current twenty years ago.'

'Game?'

'You have a pack?'

'I saw one somewhere inside.' Brenda turned to go and was back in an instant, clutching a pack of cards that had seen better days.

'I'm not sure everything is in it. "Thanks" may be a risk. We better go with "Strip Me".'

Brenda shuffled the cards and started to serve.

'How long have you been in the States?'

'Ten years now.'

'Where?'

'West Coast, LA.'

'That's outside of my experience. I spent a few years in New York.'

'I thought Laura said you lived in England?'

'Mhm. Now. But I went to high school in New York.'

'Odd.'

'Why?'

'People always seem to be coming to America from England, at least in my experience, not the other way round.'

'You're right. My father was different. Fell in love with a lady who preferred England.'

'Oh.'

'What about you, do you prefer England?'

'I don't know now.' She paused. He didn't try to fill the space, so she continued: 'When I went at first, I was devastated. Felt totally isolated. I was at a critical age. Seventeen. Time for herding and just forced to leave the few cliques I had been a part of.'

'But you got into new ones, didn't you?' His voice sounded so matter-of-fact, Brenda felt a little ashamed to tell him the truth.

'Not really.'

'How come?'

'My people wouldn't deal with my accent.'

'Strange.'

'Mhm. But true. It wasn't till I went to university and met other Blacks from other Caribbean islands, and of course from all over Africa, that I could find a niche.'

'So you say you found the Africans more friendly than the Jamaicans?'

'No comparison.'

'Did you find that the African men came on strong?'

'No. Why?'

'They have that reputation over here, I mean in the US. That's what the girls tell me.' Another long pause.

'I can't say that,' Brenda said slowly. 'Most of them treated me like a long lost sister and were ready to take care of me.' She felt virtuous as she said that. It was near enough to the truth.

'I'm glad to hear that. That's why you have to talk to different people. They are a minority among Blacks on the West Coast. I don't know if that has anything to do with the reputation.'

She had stripped him naked five games in a row.

'My ego can't take any more,' he said, realigning the cards. 'Tell me about you. What you doing here. I am on holiday. Seventeen-day ticket. I get the impression you have been here a little while.'

'Two months with one to go. I'm doing a piece on Heritage for a Black monthly.'

'You studied Journalism, then?'

100

'No. English. You?'

'Engineering, Industrial.'

'Where you studied?'

'Stanford.'

'And what do you do in LA now, beside look at film stars?'

'Sorry to disappoint you. I never see film stars, except on screen. I work in a factory and live in a Black neighbourhood.'

'What do you make?'

'Plastic containers.' Laura started to laugh.

'What's so funny about that?'

'It isn't the containers. It's that this is beginning to sound like twenty questions. I hope you don't mind.'

'Ask all you want. That's not a problem.'

'Do you come home often?'

'Every chance I get. I have been toying with the idea of coming to live here. My parents would like nothing better.'

'Your parents, what about you?'

'Look, if I could find a challenging job with a salary I could live on, I'd come. Of course, I would have to bring down a car at seventy-five per cent customs duty. David was smart. The pick-up is only forty-five per cent. But it's not my style.

'Watching them down here is an important study for me. I came by myself last week and spent time looking at what they are doing. That's how I heard about today.' He was looking at his watch. 'It is pumpkin time. My parents want to leave at half past three. It's just after that. Can we continue this conversation some other place? I have another week here. I'm sorry I can't invite myself to Mento Yard with you and Laura, but I am booked for tonight and tomorrow. I'd like to talk to you again, though. What about one evening in the week?'

'I could consider it,' Brenda said. 'You've passed the test, I think.'

'What test?'

'I hate dull men.'

'Well, thank you!'

'You like jazz?'

'Of course.'

'Wednesday night is end-of-month session at Mutual Life. Perhaps we could go to that.'

'As long as we can have a meal in a quiet place first. You can't talk over jazz.'

'It's a deal.'

'What?' asked Laura, suddenly slipping down a rock and appearing immediately beside them.

'I have a date,' said Brenda. 'Jazz on Wednesday.'

'Three is a crowd, but I have been going there every end of month that catches me here these two years, so . . .'

'So what happen? Can't the place hold all of us?'

They all laughed. 'Actually, Anthony, I came to tell you that your drive is ready. They don't want to stay till it is dark. These streets are not lit and they don't want to chance it on bad roads at night. I agree with them.'

'OK, I'm ready,' he said. 'Nice talking to you, Brenda.'

'Same here.'

'I'll call you. Coz here will give me the details. Ciao.'

'Ciao.'

Under her breath she murmured, 'Coz here will give me the details about you.'

Laura followed Anthony down the hill where his parents were already heading. Brenda was wondering what she might tell him.

Alone now, she congratulated herself for having been able to speak about the African brothers and to say they had been nice to her. After all, Milton was only one man. He could have come into her life from anywhere. She had never mentioned him to Laura. She tried not to mention him to herself. She had taught herself over time to be rational about him, about his mother and about the whole affair.

* * *

She had just fled back to the shelter of the university. In retrospect, she was absolutely ripe for what happened. Low self concept; desperately needing reassurance. England outside of the university had just revealed itself to her. She was vulnerable. Up comes this man who makes her feel she is the best thing since sliced bread. And he so charming. With these old world manners. She was sure she was ready for a serious relationship.

102

She had moved back into what was left of her old crowd. Mostly Africans. He was the new addition. Postgraduate, like herself. And single. Trying to do the LLM and eat dinners at Middle Temple at the same time.

It was a small party. In Yewande's flat. As usual, they were doing African geography with the music and she had just finished a set – Congolese music with Ibrahim, who could dance anything. She was resting in a corner, quietly nursing a sherry, when he came over and asked for the next set.

'But you don't know what it will be,' she had said, 'and I don't know if I can dance it.'

'I know and you can.'

The usual pleasantries filled the time till the music started again. Her idea of small talk was to ask him if he was sure they had enough Africans studying law. He had laughed, throwing his head back and showing all thirty-two of his perfect teeth. Then he asked whether a sharp tongue was a characteristic of women where she came from. He had obviously asked the disc jockey to play another round of Congolese music.

That's how it started.

He was good-looking. The original tall, dark and handsome ideal. Just the type she always said she would never date, because the competition would be too keen. But he wore his good looks with a certain ingenuousness. As if he didn't know. Sometimes, she wondered whether he knew how attractive he was. And he was interesting and funny. Knew a lot about several subjects beside law. Including literature.

The shock of it was to discover how easily she related to somebody whose background was so different from hers. All they had in common was colour and the fact that they were foreigners in the "mother" country. He was obviously well off and was on a big scholarship, which he said was only what the British owed him for all the oil they had stolen from his country.

They would talk with each other for hours and not notice. The next time they met, the conversation caused them both to miss a film by a young black director. She had been killing time in the cafeteria, over a cup of tea, waiting for six o'clock

when he asked if he could join her. He was waiting on the same film. They went to many films together after that; rare things, chiefly from the so-called Third World. The cinema was to be a particular ache afterwards.

She had had brief encounters with men before, but this was different. Somewhere in one of the yoga books, it said that one in each thousand people finds true mates, the other side of the whole you were born to be. She was sure that he was hers.

The sub-warden flat had been a blessing. So many cold lazy weekends were spent there. Little by little, the bookshelves came to have almost as many law books as English ones. He lived a bus ride away, sharing an apartment with his brother who was studying engineering, and there was always some excuse to stay. There were two desks in the flat, anyway, so he wasn't getting in her way. In no time, their friends were cracking jokes about how quickly they had become an item. Those same friends took great pleasure in coming by on a Saturday for Jamaican soup or on a Sunday for some variety of African stew. The man could really cook. Said his mother was not too traditional and had taught him to cook before he came, because she didn't want him to come to England and shack up with any white woman just because he wanted home-cooked food.

'I wonder what she would say about your hanging out with me and eating Jamaican soup?' said Brenda.

'Well,' he had laughed, 'she might even say it's OK, as long as it doesn't have Obeah in it. She knows about West Indians, you know. Reads avidly. All those novels put out by Heinemann and Longman. She believes that Obeah is something that is bad, because you all got a piece, not the whole of some of our traditional paraphernalia which you didn't understand, and tried to use. She says you all are people who got a lot of things wrong. Says the white people beat most of the African knowledge out of you. That is, what was left after they turned you upside down in the slave ships to mix up your brains and prevent you from knowing where you were going.'

'I mean, why do we have social history research at places like these when seers like her know it all?'

'Search me. The more fool them.'

It hadn't got intimate immediately. She had been truly lucky. She knew it. She had heard that African men expected intimacy as soon as you allowed them late hours in your flat. No so Milton. Perhaps he found out early she wasn't in the fast track. And when it did happen, it seemed like the most natural thing in the world. She didn't even wonder how come he had been prepared.

A lot of the time, they were simply studying or typing papers on the electric typewriter he had bought for the flat. They were due to finish within weeks of each other. He was going to stay on in England for at least a year after. She would probably hold on and do a PhD. That was as far ahead as they knew. She took it for granted that they would eventually settle in his country, but figured he would perhaps stay on in England longer than the year. Perhaps study some more. He didn't like litigation. Would probably do something to do with drafting laws. He was interested in the difference between the laws of his people and English Common Law, and how to help his society find a compromise.

Thinking about it later, she wondered how much only she took for granted and how much *they* did. In retrospect, she sensed a little hesitation in him every time she talked about how it would be for them when they returned to his country. Nothing had prepared her for how it ended.

The day the cable came, she had just handed in the MA thesis and was walking light towards the canteen where he would be waiting. She saw him hurrying towards her and she knew something was wrong.

He had the cable in his hand. It had come to the department. His mother was dying and was calling his name. One of his other mothers had sent the cable. She felt a knot in her stomach. It wouldn't go away.

She helped him rush through the arrangements and in two days he was gone. He had moved his things back into the apartment he shared with his brother. That wasn't strange. She was going to have to give up the sub-warden flat in another few weeks. There was no telling how long his mother might need him.

She hadn't suspected anything. She had heard of powerful

mothers. Like her friend Rachel's, who sent the white girl home and found a suitable bride for her son. But *she* wasn't white. In fact, that diplomat at their High Commission said his family welcomed his Black American wife like a lost daughter after three hundred years. Of course, all families are different. When she thought about that time, she remembered that his brother had never seemed enthusiastic about her. But Milton had said that was his temperament and she believed him. How easily that same brother packed his things and shipped them home after he had returned, alone.

No, there hadn't been a funeral. Miraculously, she hadn't died.

The letter, a lifetime later, said there were family reasons why he couldn't return. She couldn't believe that was him talking to her when they had spent so much time being sure that nothing could separate them. She hadn't gone to drink. She did start to take more than the occasional one cigarette. And she retained her sanity. Strangely, the anger was less than the numbness she felt at his absence and the kind of finality she felt about it. The knot in her stomach felt as if it would never go away.

Only then did she start to hear the horror stories of what had happened to other girls who had dared to take up with African men in a serious way. Some were telling her she had been lucky to be spared, considering what had happened to some sisters who had returned "home" as wives of these educated men.

Music, the theatre, the neighbourhood club for teens. She had immersed herself in them and became part of a totally different crowd. There was still a lot to be grateful for. She was constantly surprised at how life had gone on after the initial weeks of tears and tranquillizers. She discovered the strength of her instinct for self-preservation.

She knew then that she couldn't go through something like that twice. So there could never be another involvement like that.

She hadn't written men off. She just didn't want them as lovers. She had heard that friendship was a great institution before. She became totally committed to it after.

* * *

The cars had begun to leave in twos and threes. Edith had been mostly in the kitchen with Myrtle, and with sheet after sheet of foil, packaging food for people to take away. Everybody was leaving with a package. The mannish water and curried goat was gone, but there was fried chicken and vast quantities of dukunoo, coconut drops and fruit. Pineapple and water melon were being passed around, feverishly offering those leaving a cool bite for the road. Edith wanted all of the food out of the way. Who wanted to see all this uneaten stuff in the house next day? She needn't have worried. The young people from the school who had been helping were not only capable of dealing with whatever was left, they were looking forward to clearing it all away.

Soon the half dark of evening covered everything and they all moved towards the porch. Edith stayed back and soon appeared with a big jug of hot cocoa, explaining that she had put nutmeg in it both to help it taste like real chocolate and to help people sleep. Everybody got a large mug.

Over cocoa, David said, 'Laura, I don't like to leave praise for when people are dead, in any case I will die before you.'

'What's coming up now, Uncle D?'

'Nothing much. I just want to thank you for a splendid idea. It was so good to see all the old faces.'

Laura smiled and bowed. 'But let's not pretend I didn't do it for me, too. Note how many people *I* was glad to see.'

'It was a perfect day, girl.'

'I second that,' said Brenda.

'Everybody better go to bed now, though,' Edith said. 'Tomorrow is a long day and today was short but hectic.'

They sipped the hot drink in comparative silence and said their goodnights.

In bed, David said to Edith, 'You notice how everybody going on as if we do a terrible thing to leave England and come home?'

'Except Charley and Myrtle.'

'"You have to go there to know there"'

'But seriously,' David said, 'I wonder if they know how many years we have taken off? In fact, at least me, I would surely be dead already if we hadn't come.' Edith put her arms about him and snuggled up close.

* * *

The lights were out. There was moonlight on coconut palms, on Maas Zee's hedge, on the grass and on the ceiling. Crickets continued to make the music they had been making all day, except that nobody had heard them then. Now, in the silence of the night, the regular sound of the single chord was like a drug.

In their mahoe beds on either side of the guest room, Brenda and Laura were like children, heads hanging over the edge.

'Laura, I can't believe this place. I can't tell you how much I appreciate . . .'

'What?'

'Your inviting me here. Today was great. I don't know when I have felt so at peace. And even now the air is fresher, the crickets louder than any I remember. I know I sound like a tourist, but . . .'

'No. Is all right. I was just thinking myself that this place is like a tonic. When I was little and used to come for holidays, I used to find the nights dull. That is, after Tekel and Meera, who used to live next door, went home. We used to talk Anancy story right into the night and then when they started to yawn, or I started, Uncle David would send them home. I appreciate the peace and quiet now.'

'You ready to tell me about your cousin Anthony?'

'What about him?'

'Anything, everything.'

'Little younger than me. About thirty. Bright schools-challenge type in high school. Scholarship to Stanford.'

'Married?'

'Not that I know of. Brenda, go to you bed. Leave something to ask him when you see him.'

Chapter XVI   Woods tour

The cocks crowed Brenda awake against her will and she lay there, not able to fall asleep again. She counted sheep, then breathed deeply the way the yoga instructor said. No luck. She remained firmly awake. Eventually, she pulled on a T-shirt and jogging pants, and with sneakers in her hands, escaped as quietly as she could.

Outside, she looked down the path and to her surprise saw David already at the gate, examining a wild flower that looked like an orchid hanging from a branch that was part of the fence.

'Morning,' he said, 'had a good sleep?'

'Yes, Maas D, but I woke up and couldn't go back, so . . .'

'What about Laura, still sleeping?'

'Fast asleep. Is that what they call Poor Man's Orchid?'

'No. That one is red or perhaps a deep pink. This is St Vincent Plum. Don't ask me why St Vincent or why Plum. Walking?'

'Yes. Do you walk, Maas D?'

'I like to take a stroll in the morning. Maybe I can show you what the rest of the district looks like.'

'Yes, maybe,' said Laura, who had crept up behind them like a cat. 'I had meant to invite you to go on a Woods Village tour anyway. In fact, it looks like now or never. After Mento Yard is sleep, and leave early back to Kingston and work for the busy poor.'

They walked up the slight incline to where the Woods main road meets the gravel path that goes to the church and school. There were concrete posts on either side of the path – or rather, the remains of concrete posts, for it was obvious that there had been much chipping away.

'What were these posts about, Laura?'

'I'm not sure,' Laura said. 'I only know that I used to hear about some wedding and the carriage with the bride driving through the gates that the posts mark.'

'Yes,' David said. 'When Woods was an estate, long before

my time. In slavery days, which only my great grandfather remember, I think the daughter of the master was married at the house that used to be on the site before they built the church. You will soon see where.'

'So, Laura, the place has history.'

'You think is any pyaa pyaa place?' Laura asked, laughing. 'I could tell you more, but it can wait.'

'That used to be a fairground, Brenda,' Laura said, pointing to a grassy slope interrupted here and there with attempts at cultivation. 'It used to be called The Common. The same history book idea, I suppose, of the land that nobody owned and everybody owned. Nobody planted anything on it when I used to come here, and Uncle D says that before sound system came they used to have fair, a kind of day fête there, with saxophone and rhumba box.'

'Go easy with me. What is rhumba box?'

'Is a local instrument, sort of string . . . strings over a box with a hole in it. Remind me to find out about it if we don't see one at Mento Yard.'

'Those were the days, my child,' David put in. 'That time, we really had a community. I was a young man then. We used to have the fair on Easter Monday and people would come from all the districts around. Stalls with food and craft items on sale; Edith used to make all those pretty pickles in the bottle, and jellies. She can make jelly out of anything. And of course, the dancing from evening into night.'

After much slipping and sliding of rubber soles on damp rock and loose gravel, they reached the church yard. Brenda was interested in the tombs. She said tombstones told more than most things about history. There was one large tomb higher than all the rest and a little way off from the others.

'What's so special about that one?' Brenda asked. 'Why is it so far away?'

'It is older than all the rest,' David said. 'A Mr Neilson, some Scandinavian seaman. God knows what he was doing here. They say his body was never put in it, so it is a monument rather than a tomb.'

'I have always known it as a place to play jacks,' said Laura, solemnly. 'Let us go and look on my grandparents' own.'

Brenda had copied off what was written on the Neilson

tomb and now proceeded to write what was on Laura's grandparents' tomb. Soon, they were going up three steps which led into the church by a side door.

'I'm sure the church is locked,' said Brenda. 'I won't be able to see inside.'

'I'm not sure,' David said, giving the door a gentle push. It gave.

Inside, they walked up towards the altar, then turned back, following Brenda.

'These must be your parents, Maas D.'

'Mhmm.'

Brenda busied herself copying off what was written on the plaque. Looking up at the ceiling, she noticed the holes which would make church on a rainy Sunday impossible.

'What about the roof, Maas D?'

'They tell me the hurricane did it. Eighty-eight. But we have big plans for it. Laura, perhaps I should wait for Edith to tell you. She is Secretary of the Church Restoration Committee. We have decided to have a big service on All Souls Sunday. I know she intends to ask you to do the invitations. I better leave it for her to tell you the whole thing.' David had a way of speaking perfect English when the matter was weighty.

'OK. You know me. If I can manage it, I'll do it. Brenda, can we leave now? The next stop is the Community Centre.'

'I'm ready.'

Back over the rocky path they went, more quickly this time, and soon reached the main road. From there, they could see what was left of the community centre and walked towards it.

Brenda was reading the names on the marble squares at the foundation of the building whose mangled roof told the tale of destruction by wind. There was a sign looking down on the squares: "Woods Basic School", barely legible. She looked at that, too, with a kind of question in her eye.

'Edith has big plans for the Basic School to start again,' David said.

'Yes,' Laura chimed in. 'I forgot to ask you where she reach with that.'

'You would be surprised. She wrote the Ministry of Education and she wrote the Faculty of Education at the

university, and to cut a long story short, Deborah, Miss Glory's grandniece, is in town now on a six-week course. Of course, the hall cannot hold the school as it is. But Janet (you know, she is Head over school) says they can use the vestry for the Basic School till this place is repaired.'

'That Aunt Edith is one determined lady. Brenda, the basic school thing has been on Aunt Edith's mind from the moment she got back here and saw little children carrying water in school time.'

'I think she's even getting them to serve both breakfast and lunch for the children,' David chimed in. 'Of course, she will have to put her hand in her pocket to get that part off the ground at first.'

'You making me feel bad,' said Brenda, 'as if my grandmother's place might need some help.'

'Well, if the cap fit you, you no' will have to wear it, my dear,' said David. 'I was simply relating the facts.'

They walked home through land that had been newly farmed. Coco stalks and yam vines looked exceedingly healthy.

'How you managing with the drought, Maas D?' asked Brenda. 'Or is it that you don't have it here?'

'You see that little stream there? I call it Faithful River. That is my irrigation, and when everything else dries up, it remains faithful.'

'Show her Mr Frank tree, Uncle D.'

'This one here.'

'Who is Mr Frank?' Brenda asked.

'You tell her, Uncle.'

'Legend has it, my dear, that when the English came in 1655, the Spaniards buried their money in huge jars, Spanish Jars, and killed an overseer for each one so his spirit could guard it. Mr Frank was one of those overseers. Heavy chains were attached to the jars, they say, so sometimes you can hear them clink as you pass. I never heard them. Every now and then, Mr Frank appears in somebody's dream offering that person the Spanish Jar full of money in exchange for certain goodies. The blood of a favourite child, for example, served with rice cooked without salt, white rum, and some other things I can't remember now.'

112

'Clearly, he will keep his money forever,' said Brenda.

'Seems so. He asked for one of my cousins already. It's a big joke in the family. Mr Frank came to her father in a dream.'

'How did her father know it was Mr Frank?'

'Don't ask logical questions, Brenda. Look down now.' Laura was pointing. 'You recognize anything?'

'No, should I?'

'Yes.'

'It must be the house, then.'

Another ten yards and they were entering Edaville from the back.

Breakfast was hitting their nostrils.

'Uncle D, she have pear?'

'I see her put up one, say she saving it for you, and I didn't see them serve any anywhere yesterday, so it should be there.'

'I can smell the cook-up salt fish, and I know there is breadfruit.'

The meal they sat down to was a plantation breakfast, with boiled bananas, roast breadfruit, and saltfish soaked in vinegar then fried with lots of onion escallion and tomato. Laura went at it as if food was going out of style. The breadfruit was just a little right of ready and had the sweetish taste she loved. Brenda explained that fried plantain was her favourite and that she was going back to England at the end of the month, at which they all laughed and assured her she should feel free to eat it all. And there was real chocolate tea, not the makeshift cocoa of the night before.

Edith brought up the matter of the All Souls celebration, and explained that everybody who had a relative who had died in the district, particularly those buried in the church-yard, was to be invited to a kind of memorial service for the dear departed. A special collection would be taken for the church. Those who couldn't attend would be asked to send their offering nevertheless. It wasn't an original idea. One of the first outings they took when they had just returned was to a similar service at Blackstonedge. Edith said there couldn't be any harm in borrowing a good idea. In fact, the Blackstonedge celebration had the added fund raiser

of wreaths being sold for families to buy to decorate the graves.

'So, Aunt Edith, you are back here to make over the district. You sure you thought of everything? School, church, what next?'

'You want to hear?'

'No, no. Is alright. I know you. The word is the deed, so let me just do the invitations.'

'Excuse me,' Edith said, leaving the table. She returned with a sheet of paper. 'Here is the wording. Don't bother send it back for me to sign, just put your initials and say for me as secretary. Now, this part is harder. I have a list. See if you get a little person to address the letters and send them out. The mail from here is slow, and we have just under six weeks.'

'OK, Mam. Consider it done. I have somebody in mind. One of the cleaners at work has a daughter I always wanted to give something to do so she could earn a little pocket money. This is just fine. Brenda, let us go and pack up our things. When we get back here tonight, we will be tired and we have to hit the road early. Uncle D, can I drive?'

'No, Siree. My vehicle is the thing for such a trip.'

'OK, your vehicle, but let's strike a bargain. You drive to, I drive from. But if at any time you feel tired, you will be man enough to say so. Aunt Edith or myself will take over.'

'It's a deal. I'm man enough. I don't have a thing to prove.'

'People,' said Brenda, interrupting, 'I have been thinking about something. Let me try it out on you. There is this youth club I help with in London. Most of them are British of Caribbean parents. I am thinking that a trip out here during their holidays, to coincide with Independence, mightn't be a bad idea, and I would want them to have a country experience. You think you could perhaps entertain a group for a day? They would spend the Independence Week in Kingston, then come here and go to a few other important places. Right now, is just an idea.'

'We would love that,' said Edith, 'eh, David?'

'Of course.'

'Brenda,' said Laura, walking over to hug her, 'why did you think of that? That means you believe there is something worthwhile in Jamaica after all?'

114

'Laura, you don't know the half. I don't want those young-sters to continue to feel the way I felt. Placeless. Like you don't have anywhere, don't come from anywhere. Certainly not England. It will be difficult. Just the amount of money we have to find. But I know the others will buy the idea.'

'I have a few airline contacts,' Laura said 'They will give the odd ticket, I am sure. We'll talk about it later.'

'We would appreciate that,' said Edith. 'Eh, David? We have a little debt to pay too, you know. The pension we are living off is not bad at all. We should give back something, and who better than to the children of the children of the empire? Work on it, Brenda. We are behind you. And now let us see who will be ready to leave first. Mento Yard begins at noon. We will be late, but we don't have to be TOO late.'

Chapter XVII   Mento Yard

Brenda and Laura relaxed in the rear of the four-seater cab of the pick-up. It was one of those vehicles people returning from England or America tried to bring back; a treasure for those who lived at home and managed to get one. Not only could it seat four, but the back was covered with a tarpaulin with holes and cord to keep it down. It could hold quite a bit of anything. An economic vehicle if ever there was one. In some, the people sitting in the back were obviously uncomfortable, as if it had been made for children or for the very short-legged. This one was not like that. It was very spacious.

David knew the piece of road to the coast like the palm of his hand. Ever since he had strength enough, he had been driving that road at least once every two weeks for one reason or another.

Brenda kept staring out at the lush vegetation till they reached endless stretches of banana fields, green contrasting with the ever present blue plastic bags protecting each shoot. By the time she felt she had got used to the road and the vegetation, the sea appeared on the right and she said, 'This is the famous coast road, no'?'

'Yes,' said Laura.

'I've never been on it from this end. Always from Kingston through the Bog Walk gorge. The whole stretch from Port Maria to Ocho Rios is new to me.'

'That used to be Tower Isle, Brenda,' David was shouting from the front, as he slowed the vehicle down.

'Yes, I can see why now. They shouldn't have changed the name.'

'Nobody asked me. In fact, they waited till I had left.'

'I wouldn't have missed this for anything,' she said.

It didn't take long for them to reach St Ann's Bay. Instructions to Lawrence Park from pedestrians all included, "Turn at Marcus Garvey statue." When they got to the statue, Brenda said, 'I'll have to make a special trip for him.'

It was well after noon by the time they arrived. Parking was orderly and pleasant, once they stopped wondering why the gate used for the entrance was so much farther from the parking lot than the one out of use. Brenda noted that and shook her head, then said, 'No, I am not going to let anything get in the way of my enjoying this.'

It was a large park full of people without being so crowded you could feel claustrophobic. As they went through the gate, they could hear the saxophone and the high pitched bamboo fife doing amazing things with the tune, "Mi no waa wa Matty walla lef". Children of all sizes were winding their waists and shaking their bottoms to words they wouldn't understand for a long time. David and Edith were chipping in to the music, and a woman about their age was saying, 'Lawd a remember mi days.'

'Laura,' David said, 'the Easter Monday fairground at Woods was like this, but about a quarter of the size. See the booths over there? Exactly what I was describing to you this morning.'

As they got nearer, they could see that there was a booth for each parish. Already, two people had rushed up to Laura and hugged her, and she had done the introductions.

'Laura ... don't you all want to come and sit up here near the platform? We have seats there.' This was one of the judges and a long time friend.

'No, thank you, Miss,' said David.

'Thanks for offering,' said Edith, 'but we want to just move about and enjoy it. We might take you up on the offer later.'

Laura laughed and said it was a long time since anybody had answered anything on her behalf.

'I can see this is going to be tough,' David said. 'Let us find the St Mary booth and make that our headquarters.'

Brenda had been speechless for a while. She didn't know where to look first. She was entirely mesmerised by the little children scattered about the place, dancing and laughing as if they would burst with happiness. Old people were walking and dancing, too. Everybody was moving.

In the St Mary stall, the social development officer hugged David and Edith and congratulated them on making the trip. Brenda and Laura were introduced and given honorary

St Mary status. Brenda took the opportunity to take the video camera from her bag and arrange the strap on her shoulder.

'Remember, somebody is paying me to be here,' she said.

'We have to have a plan,' Laura said. 'It's one o'clock now. Shall we meet here at about five o'clock and see how we feel?'

'Fine,' said Edith.

'OK, we are off.'

'Don't you think you should have a cool drink first? There's tamarind and ginger beer and guava.'

'Brenda, you thirsty?'

'Yes, I'll have a tamarind.'

'Two tamarind, please, with a lot of ice.' They took the cups and rushed off.

'Brenda, there is the Rhumba Box. That man with the Jippi Jappa hat and the long narrow face. Third from left. He is sort of sitting on an instrument. That's it.'

'Laura, you have to indulge me. I have to get a close up of this.' Brenda was right up near the seats they had so recently refused.

Out of the corner of her eye, she noted people, chiefly women, dancing off stage, and she heard drumming.

'Kumina,' Laura said.

Brenda had read about it, but had not seen any but the National Dance Theatre version. Now here before her was a woman on the grass writhing in highly sexual movements. The look on her face, though, contradicted what she should be feeling. It was closer to pain than pleasure. A young man half lifted her and flung himself at her in several sexual thrusts till she stopped writhing and started to moan softly as she lay on the ground. Through all of this, the drums kept throbbing and other dancers kept up their intricate steps, some balancing tin lamps on their heads.

'God,' said Brenda, 'and to think I got it all.'

There were to be several other Kumina groups and several Mento bands. There was Jonkunnu, which some people were calling Masquerade, with the fantastic costumes including the formidable Horsehead. Edith remembered, as a child, hiding from that under her mother's bed. There was Maypole

118

danced to Mento music by little children. David and Edith heard this music and saw the children.

'David, you hear this?'

'Yes, girl. I live to see Maypole to Mento. What happen to the good old English airs?' He put on his mock English accent for the question, and continued, 'It look like we really get independence.'

Brenda and Laura ate at the St Ann stall, not because they were traitors, but because the pear looked as yellow as butter. They ordered mackerel run-down and chose roast breadfruit and dumpling over boiled bananas, and, of course, the pear. Then they had boiled corn to walk away with and decided there was no space for Nutty Buddy, much as they liked it.

Just as well. The Welcome Hall Mento Band was on stage. The group was seated neatly, in a row, except for the saxophonist, a woman of formidable girth. She was dressed in a simple floral, cotton, sleeveless dress with matching hat pressed down over shining black curls. She moved slowly with dignified rhythmic steps from the side towards centre stage to the tune of her music and the supporting band. Her face was one of deep concentration, but without the contortion you sometimes see on the faces of men playing the sax on TV. Hers was the essence of effortless control.

'Power to you, lady,' said Brenda, as soon as she could take her eye from the camera.

'Amen,' said Laura. 'What a performance!'

The five o'clock check was obviously a formality. All four turned up to release each other and set a new time – seven.

Soon after, a Bruckins group came on stage. Laura told Brenda not to move and went in search of David and Edith, who were right up against the stage on the side farthest from them. David knew Laura would come. 'Yes, Laura, that's the Manalva. See the sword dance, and the king and queen.'

'They say it has to do with Emancipation Day. First of August celebrations,' Laura said.

'We never did find out what it was about. We just used to love the dancing and the sword play. In fact, we used to run away to go and see it because it didn't really pass through Woods. Your mother and me, and my friends.

She was a real tomboy, more like a brother than a sister to me.'

Laura was very quiet, the way she always got when they mentioned her mother. As if she was trying to understand, every time, why her mother had to die so young.

'I suppose the old people who used to dance it knew the reason for it,' David added, his voice failing.

Laura recovered herself and quickly picked up the conversation again, not wanting to take her uncle with her into any sadness then.

'They say it is only in Portland they have it.'

'Well, perhaps the bands used to come over from Portland to St Mary. It isn't far, you know.'

Edith had not followed them into this conversation. She was seeing Bruckins for the first time.

There were Quadrille groups, both regular and camp. David and Edith discussed the difference, informed by the social development lady from the St Mary booth.

Everybody in that booth came outside in the open when the Dinkimini came on. It was obviously a favourite. The group that seemed bound to win was made up of children. Nobody there was over fourteen, but the boys were flinging their legs and hips effortlessly in sensual movements and the girls were answering with corresponding thrusts. They were miming, or so it seemed, the act of creation in a very spirited fashion. David was telling Brenda and Laura how he and his friends would get away and go to this kind of celebration in the village and wiggle their time away, secure in the knowledge that their parents would never know. He said his parents did not look at this kind of thing with any sympathy. Then Laura began telling them what she had read somewhere, that Dinkimini is a dance for the Ninth Night festivities, the final send off for the newly dead. That the movements were sexual because the message was about creating life to offset death. She was saying that the people who objected to the gyrations of the children were those who did not know the symbolism behind the movements.

Only after the Dinkimini did the stall and its safety get any consideration. And Edith suddenly became aware of how long David had been standing.

'David, if you feel tired, tell me. We can go and relax in the car.'

'You must be mad. And miss this? Why would I be tired? You tired?'

'No.'

'All right. Don't worry. I appreciate your thinking about me, sweetbird, but I am OK.'

They came together again at seven. But a Nigerian dance troupe, visiting the country, was just going on stage. They couldn't miss that.

'This is not just Mento Yard,' David said.

'No,' said Edith, 'is a culture feast.'

'Brenda, do you have any tape left?' Laura asked.

'Yes, I have about thirty minutes on this roll. I'll tape as much as it will.'

'The comparison will be interesting.'

'Girls,' Edith said, 'I think we should stay together this time. We don't want to have to come back to the booth to meet after this.'

'True,' said Laura, leading them to a space near where the official taping was in progress and Brenda could have a clear view.

They hadn't seen the Africans arrive. True, they had noticed a few men dressed in African robes among the crowd, but these might so easily be Africans who lived in Jamaica, or Jamaicans who had visited Africa, or people who had bought the clothes somewhere else. They hadn't read the newspapers that day. They hadn't seen the latest programme for Mento Yard, so they didn't know they should expect them. A truck was parked behind the stage, and there had been a bit of movement in and around it, but not enough for them to suspect the truth. So, when a full-blown troupe exploded on the stage, and drums and other instruments began to pour sound upon them, it came as a big surprise.

Afterwards, going home over the miles of coast road they talked about it. For David it was awe that he felt. At the similarity of one dance theatre to the next. There was no programme to take away so he could mull over the different dances and their meanings. He had noted the instruments. There was what seemed to him to be a calabash guitar, some

121

kind of home-made string instrument with a most delicate and sweet tone. It wasn't any wonder, he was thinking, that black people in the Caribbean simply cut a bamboo joint and made a flute, or put a stick through a gourd and put some seeds in it to shake. They were only doing what came naturally to the brothers on the ancient continent.

Edith had enjoyed every minute of it, and blessed their luck that such a troupe had come so far and had been brought out into the country for them to see. No one would believe that they had all at some time seen an African dance troupe perform. But London is different from St Ann, and a performance at Mento Yard had a special touch to it. They all were struck by the melodrama of putting motherland and diaspora rhythm and movement side by side.

They hadn't gone quite so far as the rest of the crowd, some of whom had run on to the stage afterwards as if they would destroy the visitors. Everyone wanted to touch just a garment or shake a hand. The little group from Woods had sensibly taken that opportunity to go towards the gate and walk the few yards to the pick-up.

Laura couldn't persuade them to let her drive back, and she didn't insist. Somewhere inside, she got the feeling that this effort was what would prove for her uncle that he was completely healed. After all, his friend Charley drove from one end of the island to the other, like a young boy.

As usual, the return trip went much faster than the out trip. There was very little traffic on the road. Even if they hadn't left a little early, they wouldn't have met much since most people were going home in the opposite direction. They made it back in a little more than an hour.

The night air was cool and clean. The gentle swish of wave against pebbles was all they heard as the pick-up struck out along the coast road. There was moonlight on the waves and on the thin line of white foam where the sea came in.

Further inland, the thick foliage trapped some of the light and redistributed it on branch and leaf as it pleased. The traffic lights became few and far between as they neared home. Every now and then, a white gate post stood out like a guard in uniform.

122

'Thank you for such excellent chauffeuring,' Brenda said, as she got out of the cab.

'Thanks,' and 'Thanks,' said the others, as if she had started a "Thanks" chorus.

'It was a pleasure. You know, I always like to serve the ladies,' David replied, in his strictest mock English.

As soon as they got into the house, Edith went to the kitchen and returned with a thermos flask of hot water to make the ritual hot cocoa with nutmeg. It was a rule of the house that the last thing Mabel did before she left was to fill the flask.

They said their goodnights and took the mugs with them to their bedrooms.

Chapter XVIII   Comparing building notes

Laura and Brenda were like girls sharing a dormitory room.

'Laura,' Brenda wanted to talk. 'This house is very comfortable and very lovely, but different, eh?'

'Well, it's really sort of two houses, in a way. You can see the old parts and the new parts. When they told me they wanted to fix up the house, the first person who looked at it said it was impossible. Then I brought a friend who is an architect with a lot of imagination, and asked him to tell me the truth. He said it would be cheaper to build a new place, but that he could do it if I felt the emotional importance of the old house was key. I felt so. That's how you see, for example, the living room and dining room with wooden floors, and that wooden archway leading from living to dining room. Those are from the old house.'

'The pantry is new though, eh?' Brenda asked.

'Yes, and the bathrooms. The bathtub in the master bathroom is all that is left of the old bathroom. The tiles are easier to keep clean in places like bathroom and kitchen. And all the cupboards are new. The new bathroom is much bigger than the old one was. I figured they really coming back at a different level and age, and needed the space and the comfort. This part here, the guest section, is new. In fact, we only built the space, and is Uncle David himself put in all these cupboards and so since they came.'

'Laura, tell me something. You didn't have any difficulty with getting people to work? For I find people very unwilling to do anything. You know, we have been working on my mother's little place.'

'No, I didn't know.'

'That's one of the big projects for the summer. But a lot of the work is careless and shoddy. Or maybe that is just town.'

'Girl, that's everywhere. Is a whole story. Let me tell you. You see the light switches there? Even that they put on lean and had to take them off and put them on again.'

'It's the very same thing. And I thought I was just fussy. At least, that's how the workmen made me feel.'

'It's a good thing I wasn't in too much of a hurry because we started well in advance. Is a good thing too I didn't have to stint on money, because they trust me and didn't complain when I kept needing more. The conversion rate of the pound helped, too. Every day, it was something else. Shortage of material, poor judgement of time, labour problems, even disappearance of some of the material. The most sensible move I made was to ask an old cousin to come and live on the site while the operation was going on. I mean, I know every pot hole in the road from Kingston to here. But I never really made them understand how much trouble it was, because I know how they felt about giving me the responsibility. In fact, though it look hard to say so, Uncle D's illness when they came was a blessing in disguise, because I was able to finish off certain things those first few weeks when they had to stay in town.'

'You can feel proud now. I'll tell you.'

'I think it was worth it. I was worried that the whole thing wouldn't work. That the place would look like patchwork. But "stylish" is the word people have been using.'

'I like the sort of creamish colour outside. I don't see that around much anymore.'

'Sandash, they call it. They paint the surface, then throw sand on the paint to get that effect. The architect had a little trouble with the landscape, too.'

'Why, because of all the rocks?'

'No. Things like not being allowed to get rid of the soursop tree just where he thought the bathroom extension should go. And having to protect the tangerine tree. It's things like that that make the place so much the same for them. You know when you have been carrying an image in your head for so long, is hell if, when you come, you can't find any of it. So I insisted on keeping those. The best shot, though, was to find a second hand harmonium. Of course, the one they left here ran to dryrot and chichi through misuse. The tenants didn't have any use for it. Aunt Edith uses the piano as well, but I think she prefers that for church hymns.'

'What about the furniture?'

'All the rocking chairs in the living room are their old ones.

I had to take some of them from under the house where they had been thrown when they fell apart. There's this man in Kingston who did them over for me. Put it this way, all the old-looking things are theirs from way back when. The new things they brought with them from England. Don't forget that they had given some people things to keep for them.'

'So how did the people feel about returning then, after so long?'

'No way. Was part of the arrangement.'

'Oh.'

'In the year, I think they have got everything just about how they want it.'

'That's an understatement.'

'Tell me about your mother's place. What you doing?'

'We are trying to extend it so it can be a really comfortable two bedroom place with a good sized kitchen and a little porch. We are also putting a little one bedroom flat at the back. It is a Housing Trust house, so it is quite basic. Luckily, it is an end lot, so we have flexibility.'

'But why she wants it so much bigger? And why the flat?'

'She wants to rent it out, so it needs to be large enough for a family to live in. The location is very convenient in terms of transportation and bus, so if it can also be of a reasonable size, it will be fine.'

'So where will she live when she rents it out?'

'You really want to hear?'

'What, she getting married?'

'A wish . . . nothing so romantic. You see, when she got me, she was preparing to go into training college and become a teacher. It seems that she never gave up that dream. A few years ago, she started going to extra-mural and she got some subjects in GCE, so now she wants to go back to the country, down by my Granny's place, get a teaching job and sign up for the in-service course. The pay is very small, so she will need the rent from the house to supplement it. Besides, my grandmother is getting shaky and she feels she wants to be near her. They doing a little fixing up on the house down there, too, to make it comfortable. And remember, the flat at the back will always be there if she has to be in town. And of course, whenever I am here . . .'

'My God, girl. So how long now since your mother been planning for this?'

'I couldn't tell you. I knew she had been doing the subjects and I thought it was a good thing to keep her mind alive, but it's only since about last year this time that she told me of the complete plan and I figured I might as well help. In any case, the place is in her name and mine.'

'How old is your mother now?'

'About forty something. Forty littlebit. She figures she can get a good twenty years teaching.'

'I take my hat off to people like that.'

'Me too.'

Laura was feeling a little guilty. As if the more she got to know Brenda, the worse she felt about having passed some sort of judgement earlier.

Long after the young women had set the alarm clock and gone to sleep, there were sounds of quiet conversation from Edith and David's room as they went over the events of the day. As if some wheel or other had come full circle.

PART IV

Chapter XIX Anthony's Jamaica

Laura did not make it for eight thirty, but was certainly at her desk by nine. She had barely sat down when the telephone rang. It was Anthony. She laughed into the receiver, and said, 'You couldn't give me a chance to reach here properly? Look how long you have been coming and going to this country, and you never called me once at the office. So what happen? Don't answer. Let me get the number.'

She gave him Brenda's number and the street address at her mother's house.

'I only want to ask her to lunch. Something wrong with that?'

The ho ho ho of his laughter kept sounding in her ears long after she had cradled the receiver.

Brenda decided against trying to catch up on her sleep, and settled down instead to writing a draft of her comment on the Mento Yard and its place in the Heritage events. She had been writing about things as they happened while they were still fresh in her mind. That way she thought she would capture some of the excitement she felt. She was pleased with the text so far. Inside her mother's house was quiet, if you blocked out the street noises on the avenue which people seemed to think was a highway. The telephone rang. She picked up the receiver and pulled the cord taut so she could still have access to her page.

'How was Mento Yard?' Anthony asked.

'Fabulous.'

'Want to tell me about it over lunch?'

'Today?'

'Why not?'

'I thought the date was for Wednesday for jazz, and for supper before that.'

'Of course. But what's that got to do with today?'

'OK, nothing really.'

'Do you like Indian food?'

'Love it.'

'Fine. I'll pick you up at noon and we can go to Kohinoor.'

'That's super,' Brenda finished. 'See you then.'

Over parantha and curried channa, Brenda described Mento Yard to an increasingly jealous Anthony. She told him he could look at the tape if he had a compatible video machine. He settled for that and started to quiz her about what she did with her spare time in London.

'Go to plays on cheap nights. I read when the weather is miserable.'

'Which, from all I hear, is all the time,' said Anthony.

'Almost. Once a week, Friday afternoons really, I am sort of counsellor and friend to a group of youngsters of West Indian background. I was telling Laura and her aunt and uncle that I am thinking of looking for money to bring them here next Independence.'

'How many of them are there?'

'About twenty.'

'Is it easy to find that kind of money?'

'I don't know. I've never tried. I wouldn't be able to bring all of them. I have been thinking about it. Of course, this is very early thinking, but I want to ask people in business to give what they can and have the kids save the rest from part-time jobs. It's almost a year away, you know. Laura says she has some contacts with the airlines and a few tickets might be possible. We'll see.'

'So that project and the plays are all you do? No partying?'

'Not much, you know, since I left university. There was always some fête going on there, and you didn't have to have a partner.'

'Am I to take it,' he jumped in, 'that you don't have a partner?'

'Well, not all the time, and not necessarily when I need one.'

'How so? The men are wasting their time . . .'

'Says he on the second meeting. You don't know where I hide my cloven hooves. The men may know something you don't know. Oh, I DO go to Notting Hill Carnival and have myself a ball, and there is one fête I always go to after that. What do YOU do for fun in LA?'

'Films, jazz, of course Carnival once a year. The Trinidadians

have a mini one there. And there is a celebration I stumbled on quite by chance, by the Garifuna people from Belize.'

'By who?'

'I knew that would catch you. Black people from Belize of mixed Carib and African ancestry. They were originally from St Vincent, but were deported to Central America by the British, who felt they were getting in the way. My history is never accurate. You can read it up. They have a big celebration once a year. I think it commemorates their arrival in Belize. But don't start me up on these people. I will never stop talking. They are my favourite Caribbean phenomenon. They have a language of their own and music that sounds in parts like our mento music. Something called "Punta". In any case, I go to their celebration.'

'Can I put that on a beginning list of things I want you to tell me about?'

'Of course. They will probably be the only thing on the list, I will talk about them so much. I am always surprised about how little we know about each other. I mean, we black people. These people from Belize look African, you know. Like us. But they are Carib, too. It's like how the people from Loiza could be from Jamaica till they start to talk.'

'People from where?'

'Loiza. I'll tell you. One summer, I went to this festival in Puerto Rico – wall-to-wall black. You wouldn't believe you were in a mulatto nation. So black, one little boy thought I was his Tio Eduardo.'

'His what?'

'Uncle Edward. It was packed. Jam packed for miles down the street. People fly home from New York and other US cities for it. Ten nights of fêteing. But I hardly find anybody who knows anything about it. At least, not among the West Indians I talk to. Language and European history have us in chains.'

'So how did you find out about it?'

'You really want to hear? Years ago, I went to Puerto Rico with a friend doing some research and we stayed on Loiza Street. Not the poshest street in San Juan, I must confess. And in some conversation or other somebody asked me where I was staying and I said, "In Loiza." I meant the

street. They thought I meant the village and that I had come for the festival, it was that time of year. I confessed my ignorance and got a quick description of what the place was like and what the festival was about. It took me ten years to get there.'

'You speak Spanish?'

'Enough.'

'Well, that's the second thing you will tell me about. I mean, the Puerto Rico thing. Belize first, then Puerto Rico. I thought you were an engineer, not an anthropologist.'

'Dessert? I'm having Indian ice cream.'

'Me too,' said Brenda, not quite sure why the label "Indian" for a well-known product.

The waiter cleared the table and brought two bowls with what looked like frozen miniature towers.

Anthony began to jab at his with a fork. Brenda was having an equally hard time with hers.

'This ice cream is some sort of penance?' she asked.

Anthony laughed.

'I like it, you know. And the excitement of finding a nut now and then. And it lasts so long.'

'You are right about that.'

'But seriously, the choice of desserts is not hot so . . . tell me. Have you done everything you wanted to do on this trip?'

'For the job, I suppose I could say yes. Mento Yard was the climax of Heritage Week. For myself, I haven't spent enough time with my grandmother.'

'What you propose to do about that?'

'My mother and I am going down there this weekend.'

'When?'

'Saturday after lunch to early Monday morning.'

'How you getting there?'

'We have an arrangement with a woman who works in Kingston and goes home there every weekend.'

'Oh. And you are sure there isn't anything else you need to do?'

'Why?'

'If you were going anywhere, I was wondering if I could tag along, if you wouldn't mind. I have never gone about with a journalist and it sounds like a good experience.'

Anthony was beginning to sound like the traditional, for-lorn, homeless and lonely child.

'You serious?'

'Of course.'

'Well, I wanted to go back to St Ann.'

'What's going on there? Sort of after-Mento Yard?'

'Nothing to do with that, though there might be a connection. Maybe they chose Lawrence Park for Mento Yard because St Ann's Bay is Garvey's town. I don't know. I have to spend some time on Garvey. After Independence, I went to a series of lectures organized to celebrate his birthday and I promised myself then that I would go to St Ann and get the feel of the place. When I went to Mento Yard, the instruction we got for finding it said, "Turn at the statue of Garvey". We did that, but we didn't stop, and I remembered that I intended to go there. I don't think there is much, just a statue and the house he lived in. Of course, I had no idea how I was getting there.'

'See, you didn't even have to pray and the answer is here. Am I not better than public transport? Listen to this. I have an idea. Tell me if you can deal with it. Are you a beach person?'

'I can't swim, but I like the beach.'

'What would you say about our spending some sun and culture time together? This is my last holiday, certainly for another year.'

'Anthony, you sure you want to do this?'

'Would I suggest it if I didn't? What happen, you don't want me to go with you?' His voice had become very quiet, as if the thought of rejection suddenly hit him.

'Not at all. I just can't believe my luck. There I was, thinking of jumping on a minibus or getting a seat in a tourbus from one of the hotels, only to find myself being offered a ride in air conditioned comfort and in good company.'

'Thanks. Now I want to push my luck. Have you been to Negril?'

'Not since I've been an adult. Once, long ago, on an outing with my grandmother's church. That's all.'

'Well, how I see it is, if we are going as far as St Ann's Bay, we might as well do something I haven't done for a long time

'– Negril, Montego Bay. We could go by the South Coast road and come back on the North Coast, stopping at St Ann's Bay for your stuff. That's a two day run or less.'

'What? Tell me something. What would you have done with these two days if you hadn't met me?'

'Nothing that couldn't be put off.'

'Mhm. Stupid answer to stupid question.'

'Does that mean you will go? I am safe, you know. You don't have to worry. And I am accountable to Laura, who is a great favourite of mine.'

'No, I wasn't worrying at all.'

'I feel so lucky. Just glad to find company to do this. We can leave here early Thursday morning. You know that road if your grandmother lives near Porus.'

'Yes, I know it.'

'We can have coffee in Mandeville. Then at Middlequarters, there is peppered shrimps. Next stop is at the border of Westmoreland and St Elizabeth. They sell fry fish and a particularly soft kind of bammie there. I don't know how they get it like that, but I swear it is the best in Jamaica.'

'You can keep the peppered shrimps. If I remember them well, they are full of salt and pepper. I am waiting for the bammie and fry fish, though.'

'You know why you can't eat the shrimps? Because you try to eat it by itself. I usually walk with plain bread and make a kind of pepper shrimps sandwich. Anyway, I won't try to force you. After the fry fish and bammie, we won't stop again till Negril and Cosmo's, with the best conch soup, certainly in Jamaica. It will probably rain, but that won't prevent us from enjoying the beach at Negril. Want to hear about Friday?'

'Look, this whole plan has left me speechless. I cannot believe this holiday. It has been so good. And now this to top it off. You can't imagine how horribly it started, with the customs officer giving me a really hard time. You shouldn't talk to Laura about seeing me arrive in the airport. It wouldn't be good for my image. All that feels so far away now. And it isn't that much time. I believe I am becoming somebody else.'

'Well, I didn't know the other person, and I am quite pleased with this one.'

136

'Thanks. I'm thinking now how much mileage I can make out of this trip you suggest. I am sure the magazine would appreciate a little "What to do in Jamaica" column. And after all this food you are talking about, a "Where to eat on the North Coast" must be possible. Are you ready for all of this?'

'Yes!' he shouted loudly, knowing full well the question was rhetorical.

'In fact,' Anthony continued, 'I am hearing titles like "A gastronomic guide to the Jamaican Coast", with credits to me of course, ho ho ho!'

Brenda was getting accustomed to the laugh that went on and on. She was also thinking between words how comfortable this man seemed, and how easy on the nerves.

'Tell me something about black/white relations in LA, or on the West Coast generally. I don't know a thing about it.'

'California is America,' said Anthony seriously, 'so you must find prejudice. Americans think about colour every day. Black and white Americans. I honestly try to avoid it. Of course, you can't. Really. But it's a question of degree. I mean, "white folks" are always on black people's minds and "black folks" on white people's minds. Where I am, there is a fairly large professional group. I basically move with them and with the West Indians around. Remember, too, you know that the prejudice has to be shared between us and the Mexicans coming over the border, and large numbers of Asians. Think of the map of the world and you will see how easy it is for Chinese and Japanese to reach California. Did you know that many of the Chinese in Jamaica came first to California, then went on to Jamaica? The later arrivals, I mean.'

'No. I have no information about that history at all.'

'California is racially very interesting. The University of California in LA is UCLA, and the alternate version for the acronym is University of Caucasians Lost among Asians.'

They both laughed, and at the end of the final "ho", Anthony continued.

'There are black people there from the Pacific, too. I saw a man one time whose origin was giving me a little trouble as

I stared at him. I went up to him boldly and asked, and he said, "Solomon Islands". I said a very knowledgeable "Oh", and went to the atlas as soon as I went home.'

'*I* have to go to the atlas as soon as I go home,' Brenda said. 'England has Asians, you know, etc, etc. But they still find enough racism to give blacks a very hard time. In sort of subtle ways, of course.'

'You will have to tell me more about that. I get the impression they have had a bad effect on you.'

The waiters were trying not to be too obvious, but the restaurant closed at three to reopen again at six. They were standing around without their uniforms. Anthony and Brenda got the message. Anthony had already paid the bill, so they got up to leave.

'What you doing for lunch tomorrow?'

'Nothing.'

'Could you put up with me again?'

'I might be able to.'

'Port Royal for fish, then?'

'Suits me fine.'

'I usually go across on the launch.'

'Wow. I'll have to bring a camera.'

'As long as I am not responsible if anybody snatches it.'

'I can take care. I'm a big girl, you know.'

'OK. Can I pick you up at noon?'

'Fine with me.'

'See you, then.'

'Thanks for a fantastic lunch. And for tomorrow and the rest, in advance.'

'The pleasure is mine. So long. I'll call you,' said Anthony.

'Go catch up on your sleep now.'

Chapter XX   Port Royal

The lunchtime traffic hadn't started to build up. Anthony kept within the speed limit, but just barely, and in no time there was Nethersole's statue in front of the Bank of Jamaica, then the Conference Centre straight ahead and immediately the sea, on the left, forever restful and calm beyond the heads of the cars parked bumper to bumper along the street. A large red steamer was riding at anchor in the bay.

Further along, a launch was inching its way in. Perhaps men were pulling ropes and tying them, but you couldn't see that. You could see, though, passengers, already standing, getting ready to disembark. There were coconut vendors waiting for thirsty people coming out of the crafts market or off the launch. People were already hanging around to get on the next, which would soon do the outward journey again.

'If you are really thirsty, we can have coconut water here,' Anthony said.

'And if I'm not?'

'We'll have it over there.'

'I'll wait.'

The arriving crowd was disembarking slowly, carefully. Soon, someone in charge indicated that they could go on.

'I always go upstairs,' Anthony said.

'I don't know anything about it, so I'll follow you,' Brenda replied.

Everybody settled quickly. There was no long wait. The launch was simply turning around and setting out again. The sea was calm with a slight wind.

'This is great,' Brenda said. 'I wonder if tourists know about it?'

'I haven't seen too many of them here. Only a few dry land ones from time to time. Do you know the term?'

'No.'

'People who either live here or who have recently migrated, but who are showing off and behaving as if everything is

139

strange to them, as if they are foreigners. In other words, tourists who are not from across the sea.'

'Trust Jamaicans with the words business, eh? Dry land tourist indeed!'

The city receded quickly. The shoreline was quite dramatic. On the far right were buildings of varying sizes and no great beauty. Anthony saw the puzzled look on Brenda's face. 'Newport West,' he said. 'Those are warehouses. We are almost there. Here come the boys.'

As if out of nowhere, heads were bobbing up in the water as young swimmers held on to the sides of the launch. Brenda was thinking how in the country little boys used to hop trucks when they came into the district, and how her grandmother used to say it was dangerous and she didn't take it seriously till George Hunt fell off one and died.

'Do they ever drown?' she asked Anthony.

'I don't know, but I don't think so. These little guys are born in the water.'

They walked off the launch. Small craft were floating in the water all around. Most of them were marked PR and had a number.

'Port Royal, I suppose,' said Brenda.

'Yes, an American friend of mine took it for granted it meant Puerto Rico till I asked him how logical that was. There's Gloria's across there. We go and order the lunch, then leave them to do it while we drink the coconut water and go for a little walk. At least, that is how I usually do it. By the time we get back, she is ready.'

'I'm your guest.'

Brenda wanted both curried lobster and fried fish. Anthony wanted steamed fish, and they both wanted bammie and boiled bananas.

After coconut water, Brenda wanted to go back to the water's edge to photograph some of the youngsters they left wading around there. She didn't know they would be there for ever. A boatman came across to ask them whether they wanted to go to Lime Cay. Perhaps he saw the camera and thought they were tourists. Anthony explained that you could take a boat to Lime Cay and have the boatman return for you after a certain time.

140

'And if he doesn't?'

'He does. You have to trust somebody.'

'True.'

'This is my first time with curried lobster and it is so good,' Brenda said.

'I am glad you like it. What about everything else?'

'Fabulous.'

'If you still have space, we can buy an ice cream cone down the block.'

'Sanitary?'

'I don't know. What is not killing is fattening.'

'I don't want to get fat.'

'Why do you think the fish is OK but the ice cream mightn't be?'

'They have to cook it over fire.'

'All right. Well, anyway, I have never suffered from street food poison.'

They bought their ice cream cones and walked back towards the launch, which was just approaching the landing area. The system seemed to work. The launch was right on schedule.

'This is better than the minibus system I have been using,' said Brenda.

'Well, I don't know about peak hours, but I have always found them punctual those days I decide to come over. Always just enough time for a little walk and a leisurely lunch. Want to sit downstairs this time? I am not a journalist, but I see some people boarding down there who might be interesting.'

'OK. Dry land tourists?' asked Brenda.

'You head quick,' said Anthony, and they laughed as they went on board, showing the return stubs of their tickets.

It was the twang that gave these tourists away. Halfway between Jamaica and America. The attempt to yank English when your version leaves aitches off and includes green verbs always results in something a little comical. From the talk, they had come for a funeral and decided to stay a few extra days. You wouldn't think people could attend a funeral with hair so many shades of yellow in one case, purple in the other.

141

And they were wearing walking shorts. The kind that had become very popular. The kind that was made for women with very little protruding in either direction. They were both very heavy women with knees that looked as if they had borne too much too soon. But they seemed comfortable with themselves and entirely unselfconscious about how they looked.

'God bless America,' Brenda whispered.

'I had wanted to ask you more about the boys, I mean children, in the club you help with.'

'What about them?' Brenda asked, thinking he only wanted to ensure that she didn't pursue the subject and either embarrass him or expose him to the tongue of these dry land tourists. But when she looked up, something in his face suggested more than that.

'Let me tell you the real service that people like me give. We play the role of parents to the children.'

'So they are orphans?'

'No, but they mostly come from homes where the parents . . . you know the word "empowerment"?'

'Yes. I have been reading a little of the literature,' he said in a sarcastic tone. 'And I have a sister and some friends whose consciousness has been raised, you would say.' He chuckled a little.

'Well,' she said, side-stepping the sarcasm, 'their parents need empowerment. They don't know their rights. They don't know what is possible for their children. You have to understand that a lot of people who migrated to Britain, and I know for sure some who migrated to the US, have never understood the school system that their children are a part of. Most of them don't know that they don't have to accept everything the school does for their children. I mean, frequently the decision taken for a particular child is not in his best interest.'

'You mean is a racist decision?'

'Yes. Don't get me wrong. It isn't always so. But white people have a way of slotting these children; of knowing what they should be, because they see certain ceilings for black children. We go in and agitate. Usually, we know what the children are capable of because we have a Saturday School component. So if we find a child being turned in a certain direction and we think he would be better off in another,

142

we go to the school to discuss it.' Brenda's face took on an extra serious look. Her eyes became smaller. 'If one kind woman hadn't put a hand somewhere, I would not have an education today. I just am frightened for the number of children I know must go under because there was nobody there for them.'

'I have this feeling you would have made it anyway,' said Anthony.

'Ah,' sighed Brenda. 'You don't know.'

'Of course,' said Anthony. 'It's not just when people migrate that this happens. True, abroad they are so caught up with the business of living, they can't even learn the system, but you must have heard stories of parents who beat their children whenever they heard that the teacher had given them punishment, as if to reinforce the teacher's action?'

'No.'

'You must talk to my father. He is always telling stories like that. About friends of his whose parents always thought the school knew best. Some of the migrants probably carried that attitude with them.'

'Next thing, you will tell me it's because of slavery, Mr Anthropologist.'

'I didn't say that. Though it might well be. A sort of attitude to authority. Though I don't believe that was so strong in slavery. My people were Ashanti. We were responsible for a lot of slave rebellions.'

'How you know they were Ashanti?'

'Well, I have a few little signals which you may not accept, and even some Ashantis, I mean the real ones from Africa mightn't accept, either.'

'Like?'

'Later.'

The dry land tourists had stopped talking to each other and were paying more attention to their conversation than he liked. In any case, the launch was almost at the landing.

'This was a good shot,' Brenda said. 'Far superior to going by road.'

'I think so,' said Anthony.

'Thanks again.'

'Don't mention it.'

As he walked into his room, Anthony was thinking about his good luck. When Leah had called to say she couldn't join him for the week as she had promised, he had felt his spirits fall. He had been so looking forward to doing things with her. He felt slightly ashamed of how little he had missed her these last two days. In fact, the last week of his holiday looked as if it was about to be better than all the rest put together. He should phone and thank Laura for the intro. Brenda was interesting and easy to hang out with.

Brenda felt she should call Laura. She hadn't talked to her since Mento Yard, and now it seemed that so much had happened since. A "Thank you" card was in order. A little too formal, perhaps, but she felt like sending it. She dialled the number.

'Laura, I am sending you a "Thank you" card.'

'Why?'

'Because I want to thank you.'

'For what?'

'Everything.'

'But you thanked me already.'

'Yes, but I need to write it. Didn't you say I should put these things in writing?' She could hear the laughter over the connection.

'How was your lunch yesterday?'

'Fine. And the one today, too.'

'Mhmm?'

'Yes, you heard right. Can we talk over tea?'

'Yes. You're lucky again. I'm free this afternoon.'

'Meet you at Devon House?'

'Let's try somewhere else. But aren't we going to jazz tonight?'

'Yes, but there are five hours between now and my date. We won't be able to talk there anyway. Not with the music going.'

'OK. I'll be there by four fifteen so we avoid the traffic.'

'Good.'

'Laura, do you know every eating place in Kingston?'

'Not every, but most, I hope.'

'This one is really very nice and I wouldn't have suspected it existed.'

'They specialize in teas.'

144

'Lunch in Port Royal, tea here, what a life! How will I ever come back down to earth? The London I live in can't compete.'

'Don't you worry. Enjoy it while it lasts. Did you go over on the launch or you went by road?'

'Launch. And it was exquisite. I just didn't know about that possibility.'

'I do it occasionally. When people are visiting. I find it very restful.'

'You can say that again.'

'So, Anthony is giving you the rush, I see.'

'I wanted to tell you about that. I am not being naïve, but I don't think it is that kind of move. He says he has never been around behind a journalist before.'

'That's a new one. What do you say?'

'I am just sort of lucky to find somebody with time and wheels, who is interesting besides. It is the kind of luck that doesn't strike me often. I mean, I was going to take a minibus to the Garvey place. Remember we passed the statue at St Ann's Bay?'

'Mhmm.'

'Well, he asked me what I had left to do and suggested we make a big trip of it and do something he wanted to do.'

'What?'

'Go to Negril by the South Coast road and come back by the North Coast, stopping at St Ann's Bay.'

'I know the trip. I love it. Bammie and fish and peppered shrimps are involved.'

'Yes.'

'I even know where you will stay in Negril. I bet.'

'Well, I don't know anywhere in Negril, so wherever we stay will be fine with me.'

'You haven't been there?'

'As a child. For a day. And I hardly remember it. Besides, the whole place must have changed a whole lot.'

'Those are still the sweetest waters in Jamaica.'

'What you mean? I can't swim, you know.'

'No matter. The water is warm and comfortable. It just caresses your body, and the beach stretches for ever and

is shallow for what feels to me like a mile out to sea.'

'Surely, Madam, you exaggerate!'

'Well, maybe not a mile. But it is like a large warm wading pool. Great for non swimmers who simply want to enjoy the water and watch the others swim far out to enjoy their depth. I don't have words to describe the place. Then, in the morning, he will take you to the Pelican in Montego Bay for breakfast. It is the only place to have breakfast there.'

'How? In that big tourist city?'

'For what you pay, it's the best you can get.'

'Mhmm, this cheese cake is good! Where they get the strawberries from?'

'Strawberries grow here, up in the hills, you know. I keep forgetting you haven't really lived here.'

'But I know. How could I forget? And I have seen peaches. At Cinchona, the one time I went there. Besides, I've eaten local grapes. Sort of acid.'

'All the temperate fruits are a little tart here. Before you put syrup on.'

'So you are really spending the week with Anthony. I wonder what he is up to?'

'Nothing, frankly. He says you trust him and he won't violate that trust. He is a most interesting man. The least engineer-like engineer I have met, and I have met a few well. They are D-U-L-L, dull. But this man is interested in all kinds of things.'

'Always was. From I know him. Not even America could streamline him.'

Chapter XXI   Jazz

By the time Brenda and Anthony reached the "Basement", they could barely find seats. It would be standing room only for anybody who came after them. Not that anybody would mind, for people were already standing in the back, some leaning on the wall at odd angles. They could hardly hear themselves think, the noise was so deafening. They looked around, trying to find Laura, but it was impossible in that crowd.

'Boy, this place pack,' said Anthony.

'Must be church for some people. Then there are the stragglers.'

'Like us.'

'Yes. Laura took myself and two other women to a place after a St Anne's Old Students' dinner where I bucked her up. But it was obviously a less popular place than this. Smaller and not half as crowded.'

Anthony went over to the bar and bought drinks and jerk chicken wings, and they settled down to enjoy the music. He was obviously in his element. Brenda tried to look impressed, but it was too advanced for her. Her appreciation of jazz didn't run to what sounded like improvisations reaching far beyond tune. She liked to be able to recognize a tune. The musicians were enjoying it as much as the audience. The pianist hunched his shoulders over the keyboard, and his locks fell forward in such a way that you thought his fingers might be hampered by the hair. The fellow on the saxophone ballooned his cheeks and closed his eyes.

Eventually, the music stopped. The MC did the usual simi dimi bowing as he acknowledged each of the players. The audience was wild with enthusiasm. The members of the band bowed to the clapping and put away their instruments.

Bright lights came on. And recorded music. The tension eased visibly. The aficionados had come back, with the musicians, from the journey they had been making together. Everybody was greeting everybody else, speaking loudly to compete with the sound.

More drinks. More jerk chicken wings.

The lights went dim again. They had hardly noticed that a new group was in place. Suddenly, Brenda pulled Anthony's shirt sleeve and pointed. Laura was standing there with a flute in her hand.

'She plays the piano,' Anthony said.

'I know,' said Brenda, 'but what is this?'

'I didn't know she was playing tonight,' Anthony said.

'I was with her this afternoon,' Brenda put in, 'and she didn't say a word.'

The MC introduced the players. Each one gave a little toot toot or bum bu dum.

The band moved into a medley of Jamaican folk songs which had been arranged as jazz pieces.

'MentoJazz,' Anthony whispered. The flute was high and melodious like a clear bamboo fife. Brenda recognized the tune and in her head she was singing, "Gyal, a wa you go a gully fa?" Her face lit up. She was really going to enjoy this part if they continued like this. How dare Laura not let on that she was going to perform? How could she have talked to her all afternoon and not say a thing about this? She would fix her when they met again. Fraud. And she was so good!

At the end, they went on to the band stand like several other patrons. They both hugged Laura, Brenda calling her a fraud all the time and Anthony repeating in a mock-British accent, 'Jolly good show.'

'You must have one on me,' Anthony said. 'The bar is still open.'

'Bailey's Irish Cream,' Laura said.

'Same,' said Brenda.

'I suppose I'll have that too. Who am I to refuse the drink *du jour* I mean *du nuit*? It's as good as anything,' said Anthony, going off to get the drinks.

After one drink, Laura left them to join the others, saying they had a special after-jazz lime.

'To ensure that we sleep on the job next day,' she said. 'See you guys. Thanks for the drink.'

'And you for the performance. Keep it up, lady.'

'I'll talk to you. And you too, Brenda.'

148

'One for the road?' asked Anthony of Brenda.

'Bailey's again.'

'OK.'

'Do you think you will be able to wake up in time tomorrow?'

'Try me. I make my living covering late night events.'

'Sorry.'

Chapter XXII   On the road

The clean smell of the morning said that indeed they had left
Kingston and were taking in what only acres of chlorophyl
could give. The cane stood tight, like close-woven matwork,
covering the distance as far as the eye could see. This was the
road towards May Pen and Mandeville that David and Edith
and Charley and Myrtle had taken a year earlier on the way
to Milk River. It was the same road. The same early morning
calm. Soon, they passed the turn-off which would have taken
them to the spa if they had been so inclined, but Anthony
and Brenda were heading for Mandeville and breakfast at
the Mandeville Hotel.

The sign post read PORUS. 'Your grandmother's town,'
said Anthony.

'I didn't say she lives in Porus, you know. *Near* Porus. Go
slow when you come to a church on your right. The road
branches off from there.'

Almost immediately, the church came into view. There was
a gravel footpath next to it. A white sign board with black
writing said, "To Birthright and Waterstand".

'There's the sign' Brenda said. 'My grandmother lives at
Birthright. About five miles in.'

'The whole of the road looks like that?'

'Mhmm. I think it is one of the government's forgotten roads.'

Brenda was laughing for no reason.

'That's in very poor taste, Madam, share it,' said Anthony.

'Sorry. You know, since I have been here, I have heard
a minister of government say he will have to retire certain
roads.'

'Retire? What a hell of a concept for a road. So what the
people will use?'

'Just what you see here. I am sure this is one of those
earmarked for retirement. In fact, I would say it retired long
ago. Cars have to literally crawl over it if they want to keep
their front end. The minibuses don't seem to mind. But we
have to pay five dollars extra to go in there.'

'Fair enough,' said Anthony.

Soon they were climbing a broad steep highway that eventually levelled off and descended into Mandeville. The traffic had picked up. The road was wide and smooth. You only knew it was steep when you watched the other cars and noted that, like you, they had slowed down to a crawl, no matter what their horsepower.

'Look at them,' said Anthony, 'like huge bugs crawling in the dirt. I always feel humble on here. Can't speed even if you wanted to. This piece of road is one of the engineering feats in this country. Another is Spur Tree Hill. You'll soon see.'

They descended. Came down into the centre of one of the prettiest towns in Jamaica. There is a square there in the city centre, fenced around with wrought iron. A large parish church, a police station and a few other important buildings sit at different points along the edge. A minor road branches off from the main road circling the town. Anthony took that and soon parked in the courtyard of the Mandeville Hotel.

Behind the hotel, they passed a rose garden and came to where well-kept lawns and a pool gave the sun something to laugh about. It was eight o'clock. The sun was up but it was giving out no heat. Or so it seemed.

'Cool Mandeville,' said Brenda.

'Cold, sometimes,' said Anthony.

'That's what the radio station fellow says: "And now it is seventy degrees fahrenheit in cool Mandeville".'

'Oh. I've never heard him.'

'Hi Maas Tony' a woman with a broom greeted him from the far end of the lobby.

'Mrs Williams, how are you?'

'Not complaining, Sir.'

'And everybody else?'

'Everybody good.'

Anthony held on to her hand and pressed something into it.

'Good Morning, Mr French.' That came from the lady at the desk. 'Go on down. Your table is waiting.'

'Thank you, Miss Rainford.'

With Brenda fast on his heels, Anthony crossed the room, pushed back heavy curtains and entered an old fashioned dining room. He headed straight for a table in the corner with a "Reserved" sign on it. A waitress brought the menu and left.

'Anthony,' Brenda began, 'why you know all these people?'

'Only the older ones.'

'So why?' she asked, wondering how many women he had brought to that place over how many years and not simply to have breakfast. Not that it was any of her business, she reminded herself.

'My father was a land surveyor for the government. Before he retired. And I used to go around with him when I was a youngster. Especially in the holidays. He used to do a lot of work in this area and sometimes we would overnight here. It is a very old hotel.'

'The furniture shows that. I mean the style.'

'Lovely, eh!'

'Lord, yes.'

'Then later, I worked down here for a year, with a firm of engineers.' Brenda's forehead creased in a kind of question.

'My job didn't have anything to do with engineering, really. I was just out of school. The boss was Daddy's friend. For those reasons then,' here his tone became very formal, 'I know these people. Satisfied?'

'Yes. Thank you. What you eating?'

'Mackerel and banana.'

'I'll have to have the continental breakfast. My stomach doesn't open so big so early.'

'You'll be ready for the bammie and fish, then.'

'Mhmm. Oh, here's a fruit plate. I'll have that.'

The service was prompt.

'I can't tell you what you are missing,' Anthony said, after the first mouthful of mackerel and banana and the avocado that came with it. 'Real home cooking.'

'Depends on whose home,' Brenda said.

'True.'

'Breakfast is a big thing with you, eh?'

'Yes. Especially when I am in Jamaica.'

'Busha mentality.'

152

'Call it what you will, Mam. I can take it.'

The goodbyes were as effusive as the greetings. Everybody wanted Maas Tony to say hello to his parents and to come back soon.

They stopped at a bakery on the way out of town. The smell of hot bread hit them before they could even get out of the car. Anthony greeted the man behind the counter and collected a round flat loaf with melted cheese on it.

'Ever had cheese bread?'

'Bread and cheese, but never cheese bread.'

'You will,' he said, climbing back into the car and switching on FM music.

They drove in silence for a while. Brenda didn't notice they had been climbing till they were at the top of a steep hill.

'Start looking now,' Anthony said. 'You will not behold such beauty again.'

It seemed that the whole of Jamaica spread out before them. One huge picture. Clouds were playing games at the edge of the canvas.

'It's just as well I am not trying to shoot here,' Brenda said. 'This needs a painter's brush.'

'That's what I always say. Unless you are going to shoot from the air. And even that gives a totally different look. The angle is not right. Too direct.'

Near the end of the hill, they stopped at a sidewalk fruitshop. Anthony said he liked the sweetsop there. Brenda said sweetsop was too tedious to eat. Too many small compartments, so she could live without them. She wanted naseberries, though. At a great price, because the season was almost over. She started on the first ripe one immediately, talking between bites.

'This is the sweetest fruit in the world,' she said.

Gutters, Pepper – place names Brenda said she had never heard, and, eventually, Santa Cruz. Like an overcrowded village. She had heard about that one. In fact, she knew a family in London that had come from Santa Cruz. Then it was Bamboo Grove. Anthony drove slowly through.

'Bamboo Grove and Fern Gully. For some reason, I put those together.'

'Related,' said Anthony, 'in the sense that you feel sheltered or hemmed in by both places, but they are almost opposites geographically. Fern Gully is like a little rain forest. Such a variety of trees. This is dry and so focused. Bamboo all the way.'

'I KNOW, teacher, but from a tourist point of view . . .'

'OK.'

'I think this is the more well known.'

'Certainly the more photographed.'

Middle Quarters, and the women with their basins of peppered shrimps. All removing the towel coverings at once. Anthony ordered from the first of them and watched her fill two small paper bags with bright orange shrimps with small black eyes and several mini antennae, that seemed to be coming out of their heads. He pulled over to the side and stretched for the cheese bread. He was right. Both pepper and salt became moderate inside the loaf.

'Well, Sir, you have managed to make peppered shrimps a possibility with me. Take a bow.'

Anthony bowed.

'Laura omitted to tell me you are a clown. How far from here is the bammie and fry fish?'

'Little more than half hour.'

'Well, this is the end of my peppered shrimps, nice as it is,' said Brenda. 'I have to leave space.'

'Drink?' asked Anthony.

'Fruit juice?'

'Thanks.'

Anthony finished his drink quickly and got back behind the wheel. Soon they could glimpse the sea. They were in Black River. And indeed, half an hour later he announced, 'Westmoreland and St Elizabeth meet here. Bammie and fish time.'

The sign read "Scott's Cove."

The bammie was exquisite. Soft and fluffy. The women serving it looked pleased even before anybody started to eat. As if they knew how the buyers would enjoy it.

'The Port Royal one was good till I tasted this. I've never had bammie so soft. I wonder how they do it.'

'Eat,' said Anthony. 'Stop analysing. We'll take some with us for supper.' He had brought foil and proceeded to wrap

away a plate full of fish and two bammies. He bought two of the packets intended for travellers so each of them could take home one. He bought a third packet.

'What are we going to do with all that?'

'One for each of us to take home and one for Laura, who I know would give her eye teeth to be here.'

'Yes. She told me this is a trip she likes.'

'Drink?'

'No, thank you, Sir. Stuffed is what I am. It doesn't matter if I never eat again.'

'Famous last words,' Anthony said, pouring himself a drink. 'We don't leave the coast again till tomorrow when we reach Ocho Rios. It will cost us a little bit of bad road after Sav-la-mar, but it is worth it.'

'I am getting to know this country for the first time. How have you managed to keep up? I mean this knowing it so well?'

'I grew up here, you know. And I came home every summer and Christmas, and most of the spring breaks when I was a student. Now I come home once a year. I love this place.'

'That much is clear. And you always had a car at your disposal, no?'

'More or less.'

Nobody said anything for the next few miles. Anthony was thinking how he had wanted to test Leah against the landscape. He couldn't really settle down with anybody who didn't enjoy Jamaica. Some other time, he'd do the trip with her. After all, he was coming back home to settle down eventually. Any children he had would have to grow up here. He wasn't waiting till it was time to retire.

All the same, he was enjoying being with Brenda, and since there were no strings attached, there was no need to feel like a traitor.

Brenda was thinking how much she was enjoying the trip and the new knowledge, but most of all how much seemed to have happened to her in less than three months. And how lucky she had been. Perhaps her luck had turned at last. Her mind went fleetingly to Milton. She became aware that she hadn't thought about him in a long time.

'Bluefields,' Anthony announced, breaking her reverie.

'What's so special about it?'

'I don't know, but it is a beach a lot of people use.'

And indeed, even on that ordinary Thursday, there were cars there and people of all ages hanging out on the beach. And from the road, you could glimpse heads bobbing in the sea.

'We are almost there,' said Anthony, as they passed the finger post saying "Sav-la-mar". 'This is the capital of Westmoreland.'

'I passed Common Entrance, you know.'

'Sorry.'

They continued in silence for a while. Soon they were passing through the centre of Negril Village and eventually came upon a set of unpainted, modern wooden buildings on stilts.

"Negril Villas", the sign said. The parking lot was almost empty.

There was a slight drizzle.

'It always rains in the afternoon,' he said, 'but not much. I suggest we register and head straight for the sea, unless, of course, you mind.'

'No. No, everything is fine by me.'

In no time, they appeared in bathing suits and with towels on their arms. They drove over to the beach immediately across from the villas and parked on a narrow strip near to two other cars. They walked towards the almost deserted beach. Structures were going up as far as the eye could see in both directions from where they were walking.

'Soon they will cover every square foot of this land with hotels and we won't remember what it looked like,' Anthony said.

'Don't take it so hard,' Brenda said. 'Tourists are foreign exchange.'

'At what cost?' asked Anthony, oblivious of the naked white bodies about to come into view. As if to prove his point, they walked past him.

'Suppose we had children with us?' Brenda asked.

'Tourists are foreign exchange,' said Anthony, in a dead pan voice.

'Touché,' said Brenda, acknowledging defeat.

'Let's go into the water,' said Anthony.

'As long as you promise to go ahead and swim and not worry about me.'

The water was warm and shallow. Like a vast wading pool, indeed, just as Laura had said. It was pale green with a touch of blue. So clear, you could see the bone-coloured sand underneath. Brenda put her palms flat on the sand, hoisted her legs and patted the surface of the water with her feet.

Later, she took a deep breath and moved through it, head under, as long as the breath held. Who said you had to be able to swim to enjoy the sea, she asked herself. She could see Anthony way past the wading pool, moving one fast arm's length at a time, as if he was going towards a special target. But there was nothing out there as far as the eye could see. Only the horizon with its splash of cloud.

The rain had stopped completely, as suddenly as it had begun. Brenda got out of the water and took her towel from the branch of driftwood where she had left it. She spread it out and was about to lie down when she turned to face two young men in bathing trunks. She hadn't heard them approach, though they were no more than six feet from her.

'Miss Smith, I believe.'

'Gentlemen,' said Brenda, trying to hide her shock and responding to their formal greeting. Then she laughed as each of them tried to hold her.

'I thought you all had gone back home long ago. How has it been going? How was Sunsplash?'

'It has been going very well,' said one, releasing her and measuring his words. 'Sunsplash was fine. We decided to stay on a bit.'

'What about your jobs?'

'What about them?' asked the other.

'Sorry. Didn't mean it that way,' she said.

'Actually, we got a few breaks in Montego Bay after Sunsplash. Some really good breaks on the hotel circuit. Guys we met there set us up. Then we had this one offer down here. We came and liked it. It seemed to like us. Can't complain, and it's nicer than Montego Bay, so we are sort of

based here and go to Montego Bay and even Ocho Rios from time to time.'

'So you will stay indefinitely?'

'I wouldn't say that. Let's say we will stay till we feel we should move on. Right now, it is very comfortable. We did tell you we were playing it by ear. What about you? How did your thing go?'

'Fine. I am going back at the end of the month. But I have more or less finished the assignment.'

She would have to introduce them to Anthony. That was a little incongruous. She wasn't sure why. Couldn't put her finger on it. But she had no choice. In any case, why should it matter?

Anthony was already out of the water and coming towards them, no doubt thinking they were about to rape her right there on the beach.

'That your pardner coming?'

'Yes,' she said.

'Ahaaa.'

'Strictly non-erotic,' she said, as he approached them.

She introduced them as friends of hers from London. Musicians. In no time, the three were involved in music talk. They wanted Anthony and Brenda to be their guests at the hotel where they were playing. First, they would all go over to Cosmo's for his famous conch soup. The bammie and fish was in the car. There was a lot of it. Enough to be the main course. There was a little beach out by Cosmo's, they said. They could eat the fish and bammie there so as not to disrespect his establishment. They might even want to take another dip. Brenda was all for that, because she hadn't got her little lie down on the beach. The boys had interrupted that.

Anthony kept the old talk going with such consummate ease she was wondering why she had thought there would be a problem. He was such a regular guy. Hadn't she accused him of being an anthropologist? The coincidence of meeting up with her friends the one day she was in Negril was still amazing. And she was going to be a guest at the hotel entertainment. Luckily, she never moved without including emergency clothes. Even going down to Birthright with her

158

mother, she always took something to wear out. Her mother said that if she went to Blue Mountain Peak, she would take night club clothes. What a good thing.

The conch soup was excellent. That's the only way Brenda liked conch, anyway. She got the feeling Cosmo wouldn't have minded their eating the fish inside his straw-roofed, bamboo wattle-and-daub restaurant. But that wasn't the arrangement. They went down to the beach, finished off the bammie and fish, and went for a last dip. The drying-off talk ran to race. What else when black people living in white countries meet? That was Brenda's question. In the little time they had, they all agreed on how relaxed they felt outside of the minority condition. Anthony mentioned the number of black American families he knew that at one time or other took off for some part of Africa, even if only one partner could get a job, just to expose their children to a place where the people in the newspapers were black. Some of them had gone to the Virgin Islands. That was easier to do, because technically they were America. It was an important experience. Especially for the kids. From the talk, it seemed that none of them intended to bring up children where they lived.

They ordered one drink for the road and agreed to meet at eight, outside the hotel where they were performing at eight thirty; before the main attraction. The hotel was ten minutes from the villa.

* * *

For a man who said he hadn't brought clothes for anything like that, Anthony looked good. This wasn't any coat-and-tie affair. An ordinary Thursday night's hotel entertainment for guests. Pinstripe shirt and navy blue pants and loafers. Brenda wore a simple black knit top with black pants, silver costume jewellery and sandals.

They drove up promptly at eight, and the fellows were indeed there to show them to a table and introduce them to the Entertainment Coordinator as their special guests. Almost as soon as they were seated, a waiter came to offer a drink on the house. They both ordered daiquiris, one banana and one

strawberry. They had hardly said "Cheers!" when the music started.

The entrance to the hotel had seemed formal; a kind of replication of elegant living of the early twentieth century. There were antique reproductions in alcoves they passed on the way in. But the tables they sat at were part of an informal poolside affair, with only the bandstand and the bar covered. It had rained in the afternoon and wasn't likely to rain again.

Driving over to the hotel, Brenda and Anthony had confessed to a certain skepticism about a two man band. But when they started to play, one on the bass guitar, the other on the piano, with the pianist doubling as vocalist, the sounds were good. Looks of genuine surprise passed between them as they joined the tourist crowd clapping enthusiastically.

The crowd was larger than one might expect at a time of year when North America was not truly cold yet. The audience was at least fifty per cent black. Anthony said that was strange, but Brenda pointed out that, on the way in, they had passed a sign welcoming travel agents from Atlanta, an American city with a substantial black population.

'When black people clap like that for their music, they can really take a bow,' said Anthony.

'You're right. Frankly, I didn't know what to expect. I only know them playing background music. They play for Diaspora Thespians, an amateur dramatic group.'

'You are involved with that?'

'Yes.'

'You didn't mention that in your list of activities.'

'Forgot. In fact, I didn't know I was writing you my CV.'

'No need to be rude. Do you act too?'

'No. I am sort of a behind-the-scenes person. Help with props and with the public relations part.'

'They look very comfortable with this scene. You all might just have lost them.'

'I don't know. They have regular jobs, and I think both of them are doing professional courses at night. They might want to finish.'

The performers joined them at the table. Congratulations were given and acknowledged. Drinks were in order. On

160

Anthony this time. He was genuinely happy to have met them. They were a good five years younger than he. Just enough to allow them to want to take some time out before life became too serious.

'You guys make me envious, man.'

'Why?'

'Young, gifted and black, you know?'

'Is this sarcasm what we get for inviting this man to hear us? Speak up, Brenda. You introduced him.'

'Forgive him. He lives in America.'

'Shhhhhh,' Anthony said. 'Wow!'

The MC for the evening was introducing the special guest for the night. A brilliant thirty-two teeth smile flashed on first. Then the rest of the girl. Simple outfit. Elegant. Full skirt. Blouse slightly decolleté. Just enough sequins to remind you she was singing in a night club. Well-shaped short afro haircut.

'Good evening, ladies and gentlemen. Welcome to the loveliest island in the world. And here, to the loveliest stretch of beach on that island. I hope that by the time you're ready to leave, you will agree with me. Enjoy your vacation and (smile smile) plan to come again soon.'

Goose pimples came out all over Brenda's arms. She was tense she was so pleased. The girl was smooth, polished. Spoke English with all the aitches in place.

'Is this the standard of the local product on the North Coast?'

'No,' Anthony said. 'This one is special. Put it this way, I haven't heard any like her before. Guys, you know her?'

'I've met her,' the bass guitarist said. 'Went to the right schools. And finished. Did traditional jobs till she decided to follow her talent. A nice girl. I'll introduce you afterwards.'

She had begun to sing. A voice like honey. Her version of a packet of Bob Marley things first to "celebrate the everlasting power of the king", she said. "No woman no cry". The crowd was joining in: "Trench Town rock", "I shot the Sheriff". They couldn't follow her.

Next came a suite of American tunes from a time surely before she was born. When she belted out "Mack the Knife", the crowd went wild. A suite of old-fashioned love songs

next. Old Sinatra and Nat Cole tunes, and finally Jamaican folk songs Belafonte made famous in the fifties.

She thanked the band that was her back-up. And the guests for enjoying her act. She was what they made her, she said. Without their enthusiasm, she was nothing.

After two encores, the guys went over and asked her to join their table. 'Only for a few minutes,' she said. Her ride would be there at midnight.

Brenda apologized for her interest and quizzed the young woman mercilessly. Brenda-style. She had been singing full-time for less than two years. She had started part-time on the North Coast while she worked with an insurance company in Ocho Rios. Had one forty-five out. Had just returned from New York. Would she be interested in London, Brenda wanted to know. She would discuss it with her manager, she said, and laughed. Then explained that a manager was her newest acquisition. They would definitely keep in touch. The vibrations were good and strong. The three men just kept grinning, totally mesmerized by the performance and by the vibrancy of the young woman.

* * *

'Six o'clock too early for you? I want to set the alarm.'

'Didn't you hear me say I'm a journalist?'

'Sorry. It's just that Pelican is a good hour from here. Then I want us to reach St Ann's Bay by noon at latest.'

'No trouble at all. I'll be fine.'

Anthony plugged in the Vapemat. A delicate odour filled the room.

'Confound the mosquitoes,' he said.

'Is there anything you don't think of?'

'Good night. You go to sleep.'

'OK, Grandpa.'

* * *

They had barely closed their eyes when the alarm went off. A quick shower and hasty packing, and they were handing in the keys at the desk.

'I know your stomach doesn't open early,' Anthony started, 'but it would be a pity to waste the Pelican breakfast.'

'I don't think the poor stomach knows morning from night at this point. I actually feel hungry.'

She ordered mackerel and banana. He had liver and banana with fried plantain.

'How come you're so quiet?' Anthony asked, through the silence while they waited on the food.

'Just thinking what heading this will come under.'

'Where?'

'In the book, of course.'

'I'm a fool. Plantation breakfast perhaps?'

'Excellent,' Brenda said, stuffing the menu card into her bag.

Chapter XXIII   The North Coast

Hotels on either side of the street, gift shops, craft cottages
and eventually the sea, blue gray with orange lights as the
early sun touched the water. They were on the wrong side of
the sign that read "Welcome to Montego Bay". Guest houses,
coffee shops, car rental agencies and, eventually, as they got
further away, bed and breakfast places among the dwelling
houses where ordinary people lived.

'This town serious, man. Tourist-wise, I mean,' said
Brenda.

'Yes, this is the real stuff, if you like that kind of thing.
Quite different from the South Coast.'

'There's nothing wrong with this, you know,' Brenda said.
'Knows what it wants to do and does it. No shilly shallying
here.'

'I never said there was. It's beautiful. I think I like the
South Coast more for perverse reasons, like everybody knows
about the North Coast. I'm not sure.'

Everywhere, conch shells were drying on tables by the road;
drying and waiting for buyers. There was the occasional
fish net and, every mile or so, somebody's fish hut. Just a
straw-roofed hut with a bar and a few stools. "Falmouth",
the sign read, "83 miles to Spanish Town", "36 miles to St
Ann's Bay". And a billboard off to the right announced the
"Windsor Caves" and "Rafting on the Martha Brae". Then
they were out of the town and crossing the bridge over the
Martha Brae river.

'Falmouth looks interesting,' Brenda said.

'Yes. Genuine Georgian architecture round here. I hear
that there is talk about taking care of some of the buildings.'

'Have you ever gone rafting?'

'Yes.'

'And have you seen the caves?'

'Yes. But today is Garvey's day, remember.'

'I didn't mean we should stop. I am just putting Falmouth
on my list of places to return to.'

They passed a sign which read:

TIME N PLACE
(IF YOU HAVE THE TIME WE HAVE THE PLACE)

'Cute, isn't it?' said Brenda.

'Not this?' asked Anthony, for they had reached the point where Trelawny Beach Hotel came into view.

'The sign,' she said, and repeated what it said.

'Yes. I thought you meant the hotel, which I don't like, just as I don't like most of those in Ocho Rios. I like the bungalow type or even two-storied ones. But not these terrible sky scrapers trying to hide our landscape.'

A few miles past the hotel, Anthony slowed down and pointed out for Brenda a sign saying "Aeroplane Stop" across from a small restaurant decorated with the wings of a broken plane.

'Hurricane?' Brenda asked.

'No, that's been there for some time.'

'Funny name that, though. Is there a landing strip round here?'

'No. Definitely no official one. I think it's a bad joke, but rumour has it that some of the biggest hauls of ganja they have are from around this part of the country, so the owner is within his rights to make a joke like that.'

The next sign said "Arawak caves".

'Have you see these as well?'

'Yes.'

'I have to come on a caving trip someday.'

'There's any number of them. This is limestone country. Didn't you notice a wall there on our right these last few miles? It continues for quite a bit. It's not man-made. There's a lot of talk about alternative tourism, or eco-tourism. It's this kind of thing they mean.'

"Discovery Bay Park" a sign board read.

'Want to get out?'

'Why not?'

There was hardly anything to see. Nothing much to mark the spot where Europe first touched Jamaica. A plaque and some craft items on sale.

'This is something else the government plans to do. Really fix up this place,' said Anthony.

'Yes,' said Brenda. 'I am a little disappointed.'

'Don't you want to write down what is here or take a photograph? Aren't you interested in Columbus?' Anthony asked.

'One at a time,' Brenda said. 'In any case, he's over-subscribed.'

Soon they came to Rio Bueno, past an old warehouse on the left and an artist's studio on the right.

'This one is really quaint,' Brenda said.

'And small,' supplied Anthony. 'Close your nose!' he shouted, and flew over a bridge spanning a river bed, dry now, past some stables and into clean air.

'Horse Piss bridge,' said Anthony.

'And so well named,' Brenda responded.

Rio Bueno ended as abruptly as it had begun. Leaving, one could see little signs and arrows leading to places to stay, near the beach, if you came for a holiday.

The sea became blue-green, and Puerto Seco loomed into sight – "Pam's Paddy Hut Fish and Festival". They sped past that and crossed the Pear Tree River.

'Is there one river for every ten or perhaps five miles we travel?'

'Yes, there are many small rivers. Hadn't thought of that? Now land of wood and water makes sense.'

A minibus plying the Montego Bay/Kingston route passed them at a speed faster than lightning. It was marked "Irie One".

'There but for the grace . . .' Brenda murmured.

Past Runaway Bay with its numerous small hotels and the extensive Jamaica Jamaica. On to a small district called Salem; Club Caribbean on the left and the Riviera on the right.

'What's in a name?' Brenda asked.

'Indeed,' Anthony replied, and added, 'The next bay is ours.'

A large sign loomed into view announcing "New Seville H̶   ̶ark" above a cleared out area. Immediately, a welcomed them to St Ann's Bay and to Garvey. ̶e it in little more than an hour. Anthony took ̶d started driving up the hill.

'This town is really very quaint. Every street is a hill. They said Market Street. Let us stop and get directions.'

'Good idea,' Anthony said as he slowed down.

Their luck was in. Mr McKenzie was a retired school teacher and had lived in St Ann's Bay most of his life.

'It isn't really Garvey's house, you know, but I will direct you to it. Garvey's house went down in one of the big hurricanes; I think '44. This house is comparatively new.'

Yes, he had the time, he said. He could come with them. He explained that Garvey had lived in a number of places in St Ann, including the site they were looking for.

He wanted to know why Brenda was interested; was her family from St Ann? Did she intend to return to Jamaica to live?

He quizzed Anthony, too, in a good humoured way, once he had established that they were not husband and wife. Anthony told him that there was a place for those who wait, whether on tables or on women, and he was occupying such a place. Mr McKenzie chuckled and told him he was a man of wit.

There was an ordinary house, a plaque and a bust of Marcus Garvey. Brenda photographed them all. Mr McKenzie volunteered that private citizens were responsible for doing what had been done with no help from government. It was clear that he expected a comment. But neither of them said anything.

They thanked him for his time and offered to drop him off where he had to go. He was going to Ocho Rios. Brenda warned him that they had to go to the Garvey statue near Lawrence Park. He said that was OK. The car was so much more comfortable than a minibus.

'Thanks for the compliment,' said Anthony, starting one of his laughs.

'I hope you never get to know, young man, what the minibus is like. Sardines. That's how they pack us, especially at peak hours. That is why I try to do my business at this time of day. I tell you, any politician who fixes up transportation in this country, I am willing to vote in for life.'

'Amen,' said Brenda.

167

'I think you are a little disappointed, lady,' Anthony said, when Mr McKenzie took a break.

'Well, I didn't know what to expect, you know. At least, the bust is something and I got it; and the plaque. In any case, there is the statue still.'

They parked near the statue and Brenda got out her camera and notebook. She photographed Garvey from every angle and wrote down everything that was written there.

In Ocho Rios, they took leave of Mr. McKenzie, and promised him that if they published anything, his name would be there. Brenda took his address. She would send him a copy of the journal.

*　*　*

They had decided to have lunch at Faith's Pen. Brenda had eaten there on earlier visits to Ocho Rios and was impressed with it. It was definitely to feature in her famous book. She had roast yam and saltfish. Anthony had steam fish and bammie. She bought a roasted snapper stuffed with vegetables to take home. She had taken one the last time and her mother had loved it. They also bought naseberries and a few mangoes.

'This is it for me,' Anthony said. 'Next week, Friday this time, I will be so far from here I'll hardly recognize myself.'

'Poor thing,' said Brenda. 'At least I don't have to operate a strict eight to four.'

'Seriously, though, Madam, I need an assessment of my performance as Journalist Companion. I wasn't joking about going to Belize and wanting you to come along since you say you are interested in Garifuna.'

'You've passed the test. I really feel quite humble that you think we can do the Belize thing together. I'm serious about it and I am sure I could sell the project to my bosses. They are interested in everything diaspora. You have to send me stuff, though – reading lists and so on, so I can write up something convincing for a proposal. It is my guess that not even SOAS library will have anything on them.'

'Trust me. I'm looking forward to the trip already. This will be the longest year of my life.'

'Can I make a little speech?' Brenda asked, ignoring his last remark.

'About what?'

'Just listen. Don't stop me.' She paused a bit and changed the register of her voice. 'I want you to know how much I have appreciated this week. All of it. And I don't want to wait until you die to send flowers. That's why I am telling you now.'

'Hey, who says I am going to die before you?' asked Anthony, finishing off with one of his recurring laughing seizures: 'Ho ho ho! Everything is a joke, no? All right. Let's hit the road. You've eaten enough?'

'Coconut water now, and I'm ready.'

'One for me, too.'

* * *

It was barely light when they reached her mother's house. Anthony unloaded her stuff and watched her put it all inside, then reappear at the door. He reached down and gave her a long, tight hug. She returned it with all her strength.

'Thanks,' she said.

'Thank YOU,' he said, releasing her.

'Have a good flight, etc, etc.'

'You too. And enjoy your grandmother.'

'For sure.'

'Sure you have my card?'

'Mhmm. And you mine?'

'Mhmm.'

'OK.'

'OK.'

'Will be in touch.'

PART V

Chapter XXIV Birthright

'Is teacher I did pick out for her, you know. Ever since. Every time I see Miss Rose or Miss Henry, I used to think that's how she going to be. Decent and nice. Teaching in the week and playing the church organ on Sunday. And I believe is teacher she did pick out for herself. From she was a little chile.'

'How you know that, Grandma?'

'You only had was to watch her playing with the others. Joycie and Peunce and Popsie. Cho. Fegat se you no know them. Well anyway, all when she playing with those bigger than herself. She was always the teacher. With her grandfather belt for the strap. Running behind them as they run away down the hill. Ha ha haaa!'

'What sweet so now?'

'All before that. Ha haa! She use to tie the bang grass in a big knot. All six root, and then she would screw up her little face and talk to them and then beat them with a guava switch till half the leaf dem drop off.'

'So that is what teachers used to do, Grandma, beat?'

'Well, in those days, mostly that, my dear. In fact, you could stay out at pass side hear the wailing when teacher Black get rhygin'. But she used to teach them, you know. She used to tell them to say them ABC, and when the grass just stand up look dumb, she would beat them.'

'You know, she never beat me yet. Maybe she was tired by then.'

Brenda was sitting under the big sandberry tree next to her grandmother. From there, she could see the brown dampness of the coffee leaves fallen from the canopy of intertwining branches. She could feel the leaves underneath her feet and between her toes, as if her shoes had disappeared and she was a little girl again looking for sandberries that had fallen and rolled along the ground and settled.

They had brought out the benches from around the table in the pantry. She was not too big to sit on the one she remembered as hers. It was no more than a foot from

the ground, with its mahogany seat polished to a deep brown from the many bottoms that had sat on it. Grandma's was higher. The same one she used to sit on while she, Brenda, rested her head in her lap and cried quietly as her grandmother combed out her hair, holding a fistful near the roots firmly to prevent it from hurting. The tears would stream down Brenda's face, but she wouldn't make a sound because she didn't want to hurt her grandmother's feelings – she was making such an effort not to make her feel any pain.

So there they were; without the complication of the hair.

'So is really because of me why she didn't turn teacher, eh?'

'How you come into it? Well, in a way, yes. But not because of you; because of you father. Is not little warn we warn her not to play with them people she no understand. For we come off a good table, although we poor. We wasn't looking for her there. But, well, hard-ears. And she pay for it. Mhmm. When saying so, me not sorry now, you know. For a couldn't want a better grandchild than you. And a sure she feel good all now when she see how you get you education and everything.'

'I'm glad she going to the teaching.'

'Me too. Only sorry that her father didn't live to see it. But she couldn't do it before. Is only last year the training college decide to do this. They say is for mature students and she really jump on it right away. Four weeks last August, and every Saturday this year, and four weeks August again. But I don't think is the mature students they were thinking about. Is themself. They have no teachers in the schools now. And who they have don't know a thing. So they want to bring back up the schools. Everything gone down, you know. Especially in the little districts. Like Birthright. Time before now, teachers used to live in this district. We don't even have a teacher's cottage any more. What we have left over school is just a set of blocks with grass growing over them and people's goats feeding on it.'

This wasn't a speech that required a response. Only the occasional whirring of the wind in the sandberry tree made any sound.

174

Brenda was thinking about her mother and all the years she had spent doing a job she didn't like, and the sort of penance it must have been when she knew so well what she wanted to do. And what had caused her to miss it. A deep sadness came over her. And a little doubt. It seemed that so many years had passed, so much water had gone under the bridge. She addressed her grandmother again:

'You think she going to be able to manage the change from Kingston after so many years?'

'Talk to her and you going to see how she been looking forward to it.'

'I talk to her already, but I feel that when the reality hit her she mightn't like it.'

'Mhmm. You would be surprised. I think is sort of like vindication of herself. For she always feel that she let herself down. And let us down, too. After the sacrifice. I believe that's why she did come and take you away as soon as you could go to school. She never want we to help her more than so. Say she make her bed, she want to lie in it. I think she also want Ivan to know that him didn't kill her spirit. Him didn't stand up for her when she find herself that way, you know. Is his mother, of blessed memory, that step in and say the child must carry his name, for she know that is his. And when you were down here and she was alive, she used to make much of you. Well, after him go to America, him start to send a few cents. I think she want him to see.

'And she feel comfortable down here, you know. These two August you could call trial period. She go up to town every weekend, so the thief them wouldn't think the house abandon. And this year, of course, you were there and the building going on. Everything just work out right. I am not complaining. Just feel glad she decide to come back home. Not just for myself, though that first. But the district thirsty. We don't even have anybody playing the organ at church.'

'And I suppose she can come and go between town and here?'

'That's why she build the little flat in the back. That, and I think, in case you come home any time and want place to stay. She didn't do anything in a hurry, you know.'

Perhaps Brenda had underestimated her mother. Perhaps she didn't know the woman at all. Perhaps she didn't know her any better than she knew her father. She thought of Laura's Aunt Edith at Woods Village. She and her David had slipped so cheerfully back into a life they gave up thirty years before. Perhaps dreams can wait. Perhaps they are more patient than we know. Miss Edith hadn't gone back to the classroom. But she was teaching. And not only school children. She and her husband were teaching a whole district. By example.

Her mother and those people belonged to a generation, a type of Jamaican she didn't know. Or so she thought. Perhaps they just belonged to somewhere, like Woods or Birthright. She was beginning to understand.

'Granny, you have any coconut drops?'

'A few little bumps inside. I try not to keep it around much through the diabetes and the doctor say not to eat it. But I make some for harvest and keep back a few pieces. Look in the safe in an enamel plate. It standing on a butterpan with water. To keep out the ants.'

Brenda had always wanted to know her mother's story. But it is a hard thing to try to talk to your mother. She had always felt that her birth had had a lot to do with her mother's life. She was a very quiet woman. A few times in her youth, she remembered a man coming by from time to time. But it seemed he didn't persist. She didn't know what had happened during the years of her absence, but she guessed it was the same. Church. YWCA. A trip to Birthright.

And very early in her life, she couldn't have been more than ten, her mother had told her what could happen if you went to bed with boys. She hadn't put it in any confusing language. Like her friends' mothers. She had come straight out and explained it all in detail. Then she had bought her the little book *Growing Up Female*. She said her own mother had used parables to her. Those were the days of parables. Not that she blamed her. She wasn't one of those depending on the defence of ignorance to exonerate them. When she had visited from New York that time, when she got the prize, her mother had talked to her about men and warm feelings and how they can prevent you from using your head.

176

Brenda couldn't help feeling guilty, as if she had prevented her mother from doing what she should have with her life. She knew that this was an irrational position. That the event that started her life and ended her mother's dreams was not her doing. Was before her time. But emotion and reason are two different things.

Joy would have been upset, too, if she knew that this one child who meant so much to her was thinking that she had spoiled her life. The whole thing was far more complicated than that.

Brenda felt herself blaming her father. He had always been an enigma to her, and would remain so. He wasn't like a regular father or what she thought a regular father should be. How could she expect to understand him? After all, she didn't grow with him. She was nearly fourteen when she went to New York. True, the relationship was easier now, in the Birmingham phase, but they really were not close.

She just barely remembered her other grandmother, his mother. She might have been four years old when that lady died. Now she knew he was a man who ran away. Like so many others.

She always thought she knew her mother. Except for the business of sending her to her father in New York so many years before. At the time, she had been happy to go. She felt privileged, like all those others going up. Especially since her visa had come through so fast. She had known she would miss her mother. But it was only when she got there that she knew how much. Later though, with a woman's sense, she had thought of it sometimes as a sort of abandonment.

'Grandma?'

'Mhmm?'

'Why she sent me to my father? I mean, since he didn't pay any attention all that time before, why she sent me?'

'I didn't agree with it. Didn't agree with it at all.'

'I know, because I remember how you cried when I came to tell you goodbye, but she must have had a reason.'

'I believe she did really think you would get a good education quick, up there. Seems she didn't see how, on her money, she could really pay for you when the time come. And she was always saying she want you to go to

university. She had a friend, older than she, whose daughter was up there, working and studying. A few people well go up there and wash plate to find money to get university degree, you know. Not like here. Even Miss Rose have a picture on her piano with her cousin in him cap and gown. Leave here after third year, I think, and go work and study. Call him doctor now. I think people full up her head with that and she believe you would get university education.'

'Then she didn't think she would miss me?'

'Miss you, yes. But she think it was for you own good. And this education thing sound important to her, because her own get stop halfway. And, you see, she did feel that you was so womanish that nobody couldn't really take liberty with you. And you was old enough not to fegat her. She must be feel you would understand when you get bigger. For me did ask her if she didn't think you would judge her. Well, she prove right and I was wrong. She proud a you. A sure Ivan proud, too. The devil. That weekend you left, she come here and it was like she wasn't here. Lock up herself and crying. Think me never know.'

Brenda didn't make any comment. Her emotions were working overtime: anger, sorrow, regret . . .

She needed time to assess her father's behaviour. She had seen too much to just write him off the way her grandmother could.

'You read all the book them that we did want her to read and that him stop her from reading,' Brenda's grandmother continued. 'Rain drizzling. Let us go inside, go look something to eat for lunch. I want to look about dinner too. Joy will be well hungry when she come.'

178

Chapter XXV   MamaJoy – student

Joy had left early for Mandeville, for class. She got Saturdays
off. That's why she had to work so late on Fridays. She never
thought she would be so lucky. She always said somebody up
there was looking after her. That's how she talked about God.
The emergency training scheme fell right into her lap. Good
thing she had got up off her fanny and taken the subjects.
She was very pleased with herself and the good grades she
was making. Of course, when she talked with her mother
about it, she pretended it was nothing much.

That first time, before the pregnancy and everything,
Third Year was enough. But those exams went out of style
in the years between. If you didn't have subjects, you weren't
saying a thing. Nowhere would take you. The notice had
said they were looking for mature people. They might as
well have said mature women, for there were no men. At
least, not in her group. Perhaps in the other colleges. Most
of the women were married. She didn't talk to them much.
Didn't make friends with them. She just smiled and did her
work. They came from different districts within, perhaps, a
twenty-mile radius of Mandeville. There were other centres
in other towns that had training colleges. Jolly good idea. And
apparently, the response had been good. Only one woman
dropped out. She didn't return after the first class. Another
one turned up promptly, saying she had been placed at the
top of a proxime list.

Good thing she hadn't taken on any of the men who had
tried with her. The woman who dropped out had husband
objections. At least, that's what her fellow students whispered
and said. That much Joy heard. If at this point of her life she
had had to get somebody's permission or at least agreement
to do this, she wouldn't have been able to. There would
have been all kinds of considerations, especially since she was
moving from town to country. Her home would have been in
town. He would have a job in town. Why think about it?

She was pretty sure she would get a job at Birthright when

she finished the course. Or at one of the other schools nearby. She was praying for Birthright, though. She didn't fancy paying transportation out of her salary. A car was out of the question. Apart from that, she really wanted Birthright. That's where she had gone to school. That's where she fell out of school. She heard herself laugh at the pun. She fell out of school because somebody fall her. You can't put past tense on a patwa verb, and English doesn't have a way of saying what man do to you. In English, a woman gets pregnant. In Jamaican, a man fall her. Good luck to the linguists.

Well, here she was on the verge of becoming a teacher. Nearly thirty years after her fall. That's probably how that word should operate. You fall from grace or some kind of high place when you get pregnant. 'What no dead no throw it away.' Her grandmother, her mother's mother, used to say that about nearly everything – people, animals, clothes. Now she was thinking about her brain and her ambition.

It made her heart leap to see how pleased her mother was. If only her father . . .

People were asking why she wanted to go into teaching. And going on about the little pittance it would pay. She didn't always remind them that a cashier job in Kingston is not exactly a queen's allowance. She would be living at home. Her mother had a kitchen garden with everything in it. They would only have to buy meat and fish. In fact, even chicken they wouldn't buy. Her mother never gave up the few yard fowls she always kept. She never got into the fancy layers that can't eat this and can't eat that. She wouldn't be paying rent. She would insist on buying all the groceries, though. Then there was the rent from the place in town. That would go a long way to making her comfortable, even after she paid the mortgage.

And no matter how she try to tell her is all right, Brenda always sent her something at the end of the month. God knows where she get it. For from all she could hear, it wasn't easy in England.

Nice little change having her so long this time. She was going to miss her.

180

Chapter XXVI To Laura with thanks

Dear Laura,

Every time I have tried to thank you, you have told me to put it in writing. Well, get ready, because now I am ready to write, not because of you, but because of me. By the time you get this, I will be back in the wet and gray. But I got what I came for, and more. At the risk of sounding corny, I want to thank you for giving me Jamaica.

I am sure you understand how my life and my experiences have been different enough from yours to have made me a very different person from you. I am not saying that yours has been all roses and mine all thorns, but I have been through some pretty rough things and while I should have been able to deal with them, they did leave their mark on me. Somewhere in my sub-conscious, I believe I blamed Jamaica. This trip home was to see my mother, but also to test Jamaica. You remember my anger the day we rode in from the airport? I don't believe you were aware of it, but your attitude to the place we had landed in was the exact opposite of mine. I noted that. And much more over the three months. It was you that started me off trying to examine myself, etc. Then the whole Independence thing and Heritage, etc, and your aunt and uncle!! I want you to know that the experience of being with you and your family (including Anthony) has been the most salutary thing to happen to me.

It is ironic that I got all of that and didn't have to pay a cent. In fact, I was being well paid. I am sure what they get from me as a result of the experience will be a jolly good piece of work.

It strikes me that you were among the first kind voices I heard when I reached London, and now here you are for me again in Jamaica!!! It is time to be superstitious.

Jamaica little but it tallawah (I might write in the report "Jamaica belies its size"). So much to do! I will never forget Mento Yard, jazz, Sunday morning play readings. I am not

sure the big First World cities have anything on Kingston. Thank you for giving so much of it to me.

I have to go now, but like McKay, I shall return. Give me a buzz whenever you pass my way. Let us knock a parata or two in W1.

Bye for now. See you at least next summer, remember?

As ever,

Your protégé,

Brenda

PART VI

Chapter XXVII   Finale

The letter the postman left was unusually fat. She recognized the writing, and ripped it open so eagerly she wrecked the stamp and cursed herself.

Dear Brenda:

Enclosed are my comments on the "Eating Round the Coast" manuscript. I had no idea you would reach this far so fast. If the publisher is as serious as you, I will see copies when we meet. I am impressed, lady. I feel like offering to do the marketing on the Jamaican side: Tourist Board and copies in all the restaurants mentioned in it.

Thanks also for the copies of "YARD" with your Heritage series. I have written for a subscription to the magazine.

Yes, I believe I can get control of a van that can take the youngsters around for the two weeks. The whole thing is such a good idea. I could have told you that Laura would jump at it. She's a born social worker. And as to David and Edith!

But the praise must go to you, the person with the idea. Now everybody gets a chance to feel virtuous, me, British Airways, etc, etc.

I have applied for leave for two weeks in July and the whole of August, and figure that as soon as they go back we can head for Belize. After the November celebrations here in LA, I interviewed a woman who used to teach here but has retired at home. Says she brings a cultural group every year to take part in the celebration, and perform songs and dances. It is a very good way of keeping the young people, some of whom were born here, in touch with their heritage.

She runs a small guest house where she lives, in a village where she says Garifuna is actually spoken on the street. I have booked rooms there for us for two days. She will arrange for a jeep to get us from Dangriga. By the way, the hotel there is giving us a very good rate, thirty dollars a day, including breakfast.

I can't tell you how much I am looking forward to this. Not that I won't enjoy the Jamaica thing. But this sounds very good. And different. I never dreamt I would be able to find someone interested enough to want to do this. And that it should be you! What have I done to deserve such luck?

I am glad your people have bought the idea. Sounds as if they are eating out of your hands. Like you are getting ready to be a Heritage specialist. I already see a volume with last summer's work and this one; a serious tome, Diaspora Studies, or something like that. I am not joking. Perhaps we can go deeper into Central America later. So many of us not known by the rest of us. I have Palenque and San Andres on my mind. They will keep. Till I see you.

Looking forward to it. Walk good.

As ever,

Anthony

She shuffled through the rest of the mail. Junk. There should be a law against it. Then she noticed the airletter form with the Nigerian postmark. She took a nail file from her bag and slit it open.

Dear Brenda:

Don't tear up this letter. Though you probably think I deserve it. I am coming to London at the end of the month and I hope you will agree to see me. There is a lot I want to talk to you about. I have been terrified of never having a chance to explain.

My mother died last week of a heart attack. Things are somewhat chaotic round here now . . .

The rest was details dates, phone numbers, etc. Brenda folded the letter. She WOULD see him. She felt pretty sure she was able to. She had come round to thinking she had been spared.

POSTSCRIPT

Chapter XXVIII   Homestretch

There were signs all over the airport saying "Welcome" in as many languages as there was space for. They were meant for real tourists, but these youths, seventeen and over, coming to be at last what they had always been labelled, felt a special warmth as they strode by them.

Brenda took the passports to the customs officer and pointed to the pile of luggage. He looked at it and sent a woman in uniform over. She said a very apologetic 'Hi', and began to spot check.

Outside, Laura was standing beside a JUTA van. She rushed up and hugged Brenda. The introductions were soon over and the van was heading for Kingston.

Shadows of clouds sat easily on the huge mountains lying on their sides and facing the highway. Soon there was nothing on the left but sea. And a huge ship waiting on cargo.

'Cement,' Brenda said. 'We export it.'

The wind lifted a pile of white dust and spun it around in air.

'A di rock dis,' one of the youngsters said.

Other titles in the Longman Caribbean Writers series:

The Chieftain's Carnival   Michael Anthony
Plays for Today   Errol Hill ed.
The Jumbie Bird   Ismith Khan
In the Castle of My Skin   George Lamming
The Dragon can't Dance   Earl Lovelace
Listen, the Wind   Roger Mais
My Bones and My Flute   Edgar Mittelholzer
Children of Sisyphus   Orlando Patterson
Old Story Time and Smile Orange   Trevor Rhone
Two Can Play and School's Out   Trevor Rhone
Black Albino   Namba Roy
A Brighter Sun   Sam Selvon
The Lonely Londoners   Sam Selvon
Ways of Sunlight   Sam Selvon
Foreday Morning   Sam Selvon
Summer Lightning   Olive Senior
Arrival of the Snake-woman   Olive Senior
Voiceprint   Stewart Brown, Mervyn Morris and Gordon Rohlehr eds.
Babymother and the King of Swords   Lorna Goodison
Satellite City   Alecia McKenzie
Two Roads to Mount Joyful   Earl McKenzie
Discoveries   John Wickham

$8 \quad 6,000$

190
X

6000

10,000
2000
8
800
—10

190

10000

10000

20000

7000

8